MW00937449

TWO

TO BE

REMEMBERED

WRITTEN

BY

MATT GAVIN

BASED ON AND EDITED FROM THE
RECOLLECTIONS OF

ERNEST HUBERT FLISSINGER

AND

FREDERIKA ADRIANA LUIKENS FLISSINGER

AND THEIR FAMILIES

Copyright © 2013 by Matt Gavin

Printed in the United States of America

Editing and design by Matt Gavin

Photography from family collections

Cover art by anonymous

Ernest Hubert Flissinger autobiographical journal,
copyright 1997, edited and reprinted by permission of
copyright owner, Frederika Adriana Flissinger

Newspaper article reprinted by permission of the
Woodland Democrat, Woodland, California

All rights reserved. No part of this publication may be
reproduced, stored in a retrieval system, or transmitted in
any form or by any means - electronic, mechanical,
photocopying, recording, or otherwise -
without the prior written permission of Matt Gavin

2345678910

Printed by CreateSpace

Published by Desires of the Heart
Sacramento, California, USA

DEDICATION

This book is dedicated to all the Dutch East Indies victims and their families who suffered the hardships, atrocities, and devastation of World War II and the subsequent Indonesian uprising. May their lives and experiences never be forgotten.

CONTENTS

ACKNOWLEDGEMENTS

I recognize and greatly appreciate the abundant contributions of all those involved in the writing and publishing of this book.

Special gratitude goes to:

Ernest and Frederika Flissinger, of course, whose obvious satisfaction, relish, and sometimes solace in recounting and reiterating their life experiences to their family over the course of many, many years was the inspiration for this book;

My wife, Marguerite J. Flissinger-Gavin, the family historian, whose efforts through the years to recall and document and photograph and videotape her parents' lives, whose fortuitous insistence on videotaping interviews with her parents shortly before her father passed, whose proofreading and assistance with content and choice of photographs, and, above all, whose drive to ensure that Ernest and Frederika's story was printed for posterity, were monumental in making this book a reality;

Raymond Flissinger, whose personal recollections and the typing of Ernest's memoirs were a boon to my efforts;

Wolter and Nora van der Torren, whose remembrances of their own lives and parallel experiences provided historical corroboration;

In Australia, Jennifer Ann Flissinger Hasler, whose assistance in gathering records and providing contacts with regard to the Australian branches of the family was extremely helpful;

Also in Australia, Irene Flissinger and Jenny Flissinger who were able to provide answers to lingering questions; and

In The Netherlands, Peter Luikens, Paul Hendriks, Sonja van der Torren, Patricia Flissinger Kok, and Frans Flissinger who helped fill in a number of time frame and genealogical blanks.

I would like to express an additional thank you to all who provided or offered photographs for this account. It is a joy to know that there are such wonderful pictorial artifacts of family members from long ago that will keep their beautiful countenances alive for future generations. Whereas there were a number of photos we did not choose to use, each one was considered and appreciated. Marguerite and I meticulously selected each photo with the hope that it will provide the reader with the appropriate and timely image to carry this compelling story forward. And certainly Marguerite's imaginative capturing of her mother in a present-day moment is a fitting close for the book.

MG

I want to give many, many thanks with great love and admiration to my husband, Matt, for all the hours, days, weeks, and months - nearly a whole year - he dedicated to writing this book. If it were not for his professionalism, hard work, and talent, my parents' incredible story would likely have been lost with time. Now, for many generations to come, our family, as well as other readers, will know the sacrifices and choices that were made to keep the Flissinger-Luikens tree flourishing.

Mom and Pop, this book was written for you with love and respect and admiration for what you have gone through in your lives. You have overcome so many tribulations, sad and horrific situations, and fears of an unknown future, and yet you forever strove to do the best for each other, your children and their families, your relatives, and your friends. You made a beautiful life for my three brothers and me. Mom and Pop, we love you both so very much and we present this book to you as an expression of our everlasting gratitude.

Marguerite J. Flissinger-Gavin

AUTHOR'S NOTES

My objective in this book is twofold: to document as much of Ernest and Frederika's Dutch-Indonesian history as possible, and also to record the genealogies of the Flissinger and Luikens families. As it has been many decades since their experiences took place, the accuracy of facts, names, dates, and places was sometimes in question. I went to lengths to corroborate the information but possibly may have fallen short in some instances. If so, apologies are extended for any historical inaccuracies, omissions, or errors, but these accounts, descriptions, and particulars are as correct as Ernest, Frederika, and their families' documents, papers, and memories and my research could establish.

With regard to the genealogies, I have gone as far back as family information can be corroborated, and I found it logical to carry the story forward essentially only as far as the generation that succeeded Ernest, Frederika, and their siblings, for many of those offspring experienced a portion of the Dutch-Indonesian years.

I am aware that it is not always easy to follow a genealogy. I have done my utmost to be as descriptive and clear as possible so that the reader is not confused by names and relationships, but, as with many families, names - first names in particular - are often duplicated from one generation to another. I trust that the family lineages in the

Appendixes section will provide additional clarity.

Included in the book are transcriptions of taped interviews with Ernest and Frederika. Quotes from such are indicated by initials and a colon and are italicized as follows:

EF: (Ernest Flissinger)

FF: (Frederika Luikens Flissinger)

MFG: (Marguerite Flissinger-Gavin, daughter)

MG: (Matt Gavin, son-in-law, author)

Also included is most of Ernest's autobiographical journal the majority of which he penned to paper in the late 1990s. Each portion herein is indicated by use of this font and indentation.

Ernest Flissinger was a kind, considerate, loving, and compassionate man. As he states in his writings, he did not grow up with prejudice and he interacted regularly with people of many different races. It is apparent, however, from what he wrote and from his verbal accounts that during the war he felt great animosity for the Japanese invaders. Whereas political correctness today would suggest otherwise, I have chosen for historical accuracy to quote Ernest verbatim in his use of the pejorative term "Japs" when he spoke of the Japanese during those horrific times. It is understandable why he and so many others worldwide expressed their disdain profanely back then.

As I have striven to relate the events of this epic in chronological sequence, I have made use of asterisks to connote changes in the direction of the story:

∗∗

Two asterisks merely indicate that the narrative stops and starts anew on a different topic;

∗∗∗∗

Four asterisks denote a switch from one family member to another;

∗∗∗∗∗∗

Six asterisks shift the chronicle from one lineage to the other (e.g. Flissinger to Luikens.).

Those living in the Dutch East Indies encountered not only the native languages of Dutch and Indonesian but a multitude of other languages and local dialects, as the archipelago had been a melting pot of world travelers for centuries. Consequently, some words herein, unfamiliar to many readers, are as correct and corroborated as I could determine and were selected with contemporary readership in mind.

In the more than half a century that Ernest and Frederika have lived in America their use of English has shown remarkable accuracy and fluency. However, it is quite understandable that, coming from such a diverse environment and never having completely lost their Dutch accents, they have not always been perfect in speaking or writing their newest acquired language. Consequently, I have edited their narratives when more clarity seemed appropriate but I also have often quoted them verbatim to give the reader the flavor of their mosaic personalities.

PREFACE

The lives of Ernest Hubert Flissinger and Frederika Adriana Luikens Flissinger are - certainly from their family's viewpoint - extraordinary, courageous, inspiring, and most definitely worthy of historic note. From childhoods in a tropical paradise to the fruition of the American dream, this couple survived and succeeded on intelligence, inner strength, good fortune, guts, drive, and nobility.

This is their chronicle as gleaned from the many stories they told, the emotional reminiscences they shared through the years, taped interviews in 2006 (with Ernest and Frederika) and 2013 (with Frederika), family records, papers, and letters, and autobiographical notes and writings.

Ernest, fondly called Nes, and Frederika, fondly called Riek or Rika, lived long, productive, and prosperous lives. But so much could have altered their history.

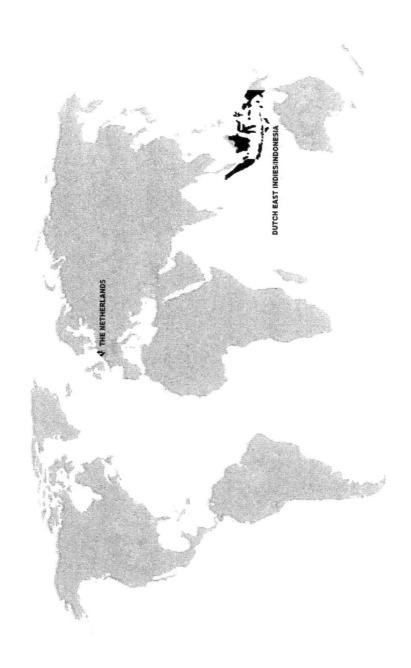

THE NETHERLANDS

DUTCH EAST INDIES/INDONESIA

INTRODUCTION

To most Americans and perhaps many others around the world the archipelago of Indonesia is a distant notion of relatively unimportant islands somewhere in the Pacific. Perhaps a vague remembrance from bygone schooldays conjures up trading ships and spices and brown-skinned natives on highly vegetative landscapes. But in reality Indonesia has been much more significant to world history and the growth of nations than most schoolbooks have acknowledged. So, as we tell the Flissinger-Luikens story, some historical background will lend a perspective.

It was in the late 1400s that Portuguese seamen first sailed to these remote islands. News of commercial possibilities spread throughout Europe and gradually trade routes were established by Portugal and other seafaring nations, in particular England and, by 1595, The Netherlands. As various Dutch groups were vying for the same lucrative spice products, The Netherlands government amalgamated the competitors into one enterprise called the Vereenigde Oost-Indishe Compagnie (United East India Company) or VOC, and granted the VOC a charter to make treaties, establish settlements, and wage war, as necessary, in order to firm up the Dutch hold on spice trading with Asia. A major result of these endeavors was the colonization of much of Indonesia under Dutch rule, with a capital set up in the seaport city of Batavia (now Jakarta) on the northwest coast of the island of Java.

Java is the world's thirteenth largest island and sits about 700 miles south of the Equator and 1200 miles northwest of Australia. Its 650 mile length and 130 mile width were formed by a string of volcanos which now accentuates the topography from east to west through the middle of the land mass. Java's terrain spreads from the stark volcanic mountains through tropical jungles and rainforests to the lush coastal regions. The rainy season of November to June is followed by the much dryer months of July to October. Very comfortable temperatures range from 72 to 90 degrees most of the year, though the average 75% humidity detracts a bit from the island's paradisiacal perfection.

For two hundred years the VOC governed and profited. But in the late 1700s, due to the cost of mismanagement, corruption, smuggling, and wars, the VOC filed bankruptcy. In 1800 the company was formally dissolved and The Netherlands government nationalized the colonies, calling them the Dutch East Indies. Fortunately the production and trade of indigenous spices (nutmeg, mace spice, cloves, cinnamon) plus introduced, non-indigenous cash crops (coffee, tea, cacao, tobacco, rubber, sugar) continued extremely profitably for another century, making The Netherlands one of the world's great colonial powers. Further gains were realized when the oil industry began production there in the late 1800s. Because of the colonization and good employment opportunities in the lucrative businesses, many Dutch and other Europeans were enticed to relocate to the islands.

1.

THE HEAD OF THE LINE

Sometime during the Dutch colonial period, the date unknown, the first Flissinger arrived in Indonesia. It seems highly probable that he came from the town of Vlissingen, a seaport village in The Netherlands, where ships were built and set sail for the Far East. And at some point the V in Vlissingen may have inadvertently or purposely been changed to an F when speaking of said port, and it is believed that Flissinger is a shortened version of the original name, von Flissinger - "von" meaning "of".

Ernest Flissinger lived with the understanding that his family blood line was a combination of Dutch and Indonesian, so it is likely that somewhere up the lineage a Flissinger married an Indonesian woman or perhaps a Dutch woman of mixed blood. Ernest made reference to his father as a "mixture" and reference to his paternal grandmother as a "mixture".

At this writing in the year 2013 the oldest Flissinger ancestor known to the family is Ernest's paternal great-grandfather, Anthony Coenraad Flissinger, born in 1831 in Surabaya, East Java. He married (date unknown) Hendrika Christina Cramer and they begot six children (chronology unknown): Antoinette Flissinger, Dora Flissinger, Heinrich Flissinger, Marie Flissinger, Ketelaar Flissinger, and

Frederich Wilhelm Flissinger who would be Ernest's grandfather. Anthony lived to be fifty-two, passing in 1883.

Frederich (Opa [grandpa] Pede, to Ernest) was also born in Surabaya, on December 15, 1862. He married Rosalie Cramer (Oma [grandma] Rose, to Ernest), born October 22, 1867, in a town near Surabaya called Modjokerto. She was the daughter of a Dutchman, Elias Antonius Cramer (1833-1891), and his wife, an Indonesian woman known to the family as Ma Bre (1839-1893).

Ernest recalls this from his childhood:

> *EF: Oma Rose and Opa Pede got married and what I remember being told was their marriage was not too good and they split up, but they remarried. Oma was harsh sometimes with her mouth and Opa was a soft-spoken, easy-going man. But later they got along very well together.*

Indeed Frederich and Rosalie married on May 5, 1884, divorced in 1902, and remarried on March 21, 1923. To them were born perhaps as many as seven or eight children. Family notes indicate the names of five: Eduard Flissinger, Laurence Flissinger, Jeanne Flissinger, Jan Flissinger, and Frans Willem Flissinger, who would be Ernest's father, born in Surabaya on June 8, 1888.

****

On Ernest's maternal side his grandfather was Jacobus Petrus Broens, born July 25, 1858, in The Netherlands where he married a woman of German descent, Adriana Jacoba Agatha Calvis (known as Agatha), born July 25, 1863. In Delft, The Netherlands, on June 11, 1892, a daughter, Martina Jacoba Adriana Broens, was born. She would be Ernest's mother. For reasons unknown - perhaps a career opportunity - the Broenses relocated to East Java, Indonesia in 1899.

Sadly, Ernest would never know his maternal grandparents. Though little is remembered about this Broens family, Ernest relates:

> *EF: My mother grew up in that area* [East Java] *and she was fluent in the local language which was Javanese, and even the natives couldn't tell the difference when they were speaking with her - whether they were speaking to a native or someone else. But she was Dutch, she came to Indie with her parents, as a girl of seven, and her father worked with the railroads. One day on the job he got impatient - he was a heavy-built man, a real Dutchman - and he got impatient with the locals because they could not move a lorry wheel. He showed them how to do it and he had a heart attack there. Broke a vein in his neck. He died there. So my grandmother Broens brought up her daughter (my mother) by herself.*

The year was 1900 when Jacobus Petrus Broens died at the age of forty-two, only a year after arriving in Java. Nevertheless, during this new century's first decade Martina grew into a flourishing teenager.

MFG: Was your mother an only child?

EF: As far as I know. We haven't heard of any brothers or sisters that she had.

But Martina was not without companionship. At some serendipitous moment Frans Flissinger, four years her senior, had entered her life. The Flissinger and Broens families both lived in Surabaya and although the circumstances of the young couple's courtship have not been passed down, Frans and Martina married in that city in 1909. Frans, however, was not happy there.

> *EF: Oma Rose couldn't manage her money so well and at that time the schools had to be paid for - they were government schools. Frans (my father) was so embarrassed that the administrators were always asking for money that he quit school. But he was a self-made young man - he spoke several languages - and [in 1908] he secured himself a job with the post office.*

As a young couple Frans and Martina moved to West Java, living in Batavia, towns west of there, and also in Sumatra, likely wherever postal employment took Frans.

MFG: Your father had brothers and sisters?

EF: He had very many brothers and sisters - seven, I think. Oom [uncle] Lau was one of them and a sister I met and another brother I met - Oom Jan. The others I never met. We were personally not close. We lived on the west side of

Java and those folks lived on the east. That's why we never kept in contact with the family from the east. And we had a different culture from the people there. Java is divided into three parts - east, middle, and west - and all those sections have different populations, different languages, different cultures, different kinds of food - all is different.

For the newlyweds in the west the Fates were not kind. On March 22, 1910, Martina's mother, Agatha Calvis Broens, passed away in Surabaya at age forty-six. With no one left on her side of the family, Martina, one could suppose, was eager to have a family of her own. But it was a struggle.

EF: I had two sisters who died in Atjeh, in northern Sumatra, before I was born. Fransje [Frances Flissinger] was the oldest. She died at the age of seven of typhoid fever. The doctor was called but he couldn't make it on time because the transportation was over water by boat. And Agatha [Agatha Flissinger] died at the age of one - what the reason of her death was, I do not know. It seemed to have affected my mother tremendously.

FF: All the girls that she bore died.

But reward was still in store for this family.

2.

ACROSS THE SEAS

Meanwhile the family Luikens had been producing its own lineage far and near. Frederika's paternal grandfather was Wolter Lukens (original spelling), born in 1837 in the small village of Pekela in Groningen Province, The Netherlands. He was the son of a minister in the Protestant Reformed Church. Born in the same village on October 15, 1840, was Japier Nieboer, the woman Wolter married on February 2, 1860. There in Pekela they begot two daughters and two sons, one of which was Johannes Lukens, born November 30, 1865, who would be Frederika's father.

Wolter was for a number of years a sea captain sailing Dutch commercial vessels to and from South America. As was often allowed, Japier accompanied Wolter on some of his voyages. Unfortunately, during a stay in Rio de Janeiro, Japier contracted yellow fever and passed away. Later, it is reputed, Wolter emigrated to America, perhaps to Chicago, and married an American or English woman.

After coming of age, Wolter's son, Johannes, joined the Dutch military and was apparently reassigned (year unknown) to the Dutch East Indies.

****

On her mother's side Frederika's great-grandfather was

Franciscus Jacobus de la Fonteyne, born October 3, 1832, in Vlissingen, The Netherlands. He, too, was a military man, and, after reassignment (year unknown) to the Dutch East Indies, he married an Indonesian woman named Siela.

> *FF: He fought the wars in Borneo and Sumatra and that's where [Sumatra] he married and got his two children, a boy and a girl.*

But during one of those wars Siela was murdered. Franciscus chose to put the two children in an orphanage. He then returned to The Netherlands where he eventually married a woman, surname Ross, it is believed.

> *FF: I remember my grandfather on my mother's side. The orphaned boy is my grandfather, Franciscus Anton Everhard de la Fonteyne [born February 16, 1856, in Sambas, Borneo], and the girl, Frederika de la Fonteyne - they don't know what happened to her.*

Young Franciscus grew up to serve also in the Dutch military there in the Dutch East Indies, attaining the rank of sergeant. He married Albertina Carolina Herman, a Dutch woman born April 22, 1861, in Ambarawa, Java. They gave birth to two boys and three girls. The second child was Marie Jacqueline de la Fonteyne, who would be Frederika's mother. She was born in Batavia, January 16, 1883.

Family notes indicate Marie's siblings were Albertina de la Fonteyne, Frederick Eduard de la Fonteyne, Sophia Helena de la Fonteyne, and Alexius de la Fonteyne.

Albertina Carolina Herman de la Fonteyne passed away at the age of forty in Batavia on August 1, 1901, when Marie was eighteen. Then, as destiny would have it, three lives serendipitously intersected.

> *FF: My father, Johannes Luikens* [spelling changed from Lukens, date and reason unknown]*, was in the military for a while and that is where he met my grandfather, Franciscus de la Fonteyne, who, at some point, introduced Johannes to his daughter, Marie, my mother.*

Marie and Johannes married in 1902 in Batavia. Switching careers into the private sector, Johannes took a position with BPM (Batavia Petroleum Maatschappij [company]).

It is informative to note here that, to compete with America's then dominant Standard Oil, the Royal Dutch

Petroleum Company merged in 1907 with Shell Transport and Trading Company of the United Kingdom, forming The Royal Dutch Shell Group which encompassed the already established (1869) Batavia Petroleum Company. Oil had become Indonesia's most important mineral resource with extensive production in Sumatra, Java, and Kalimantan. Johannes, now a Shell employee, was assigned to oil-plentiful Sumatra.

3.

BOUNTIFUL BLESSINGS

In Palembang, Sumatra, Johannes and Marie Luikens were prolific in progeny. In an eleven year period they had six children.

FF: I had one brother and four sisters.

MG: In what order did they come?

FF: Moeske [Moes, for short] - *that was just the name they gave her, but her real name was Albertine Hermanna Luikens* [born July 8, 1905, in a hospital is Batavia].
And then the second child was Maria (called Marie) Johanna Luikens. She was born in 1907 [June 2].
Then after Marie came my brother, Wolter Franciscus Luikens, born in 1909 [August 27].
Then after him I had a sister, Sophia [Fiet or Fietje, for short] *Antonia Luikens* [born August 1, 1911].
Two years later there came Johanna [Joop or Jopie, for short] *Jacoba Luikens, born in 1913* [November 8].

It has been presumed from the children's wearing of the sashes (sjerps) around their waists that this photo was taken on August 31, 1915, in celebration of Queen (of The Netherlands) Wilhelmina's birthday.

Frederika's subsequent arrival as the last of these half-dozen youngsters turned out to be a bit more fascinating.

For many years it was the policy of the government of The Netherlands to grant Dutch employees in the East Indies colony an eight-month paid furlough back to the home country after every six years of employment. The employee's whole family (sometimes including a servant) was provided this vacation.

In early 1910 Johannes and Marie and their first three children, Moes, Marie, and Wolter, made their initial furlough voyage to The Netherlands, returning in late October. In 1916 the Luikenses, then with two more daughters, Fietje and Jopie, enjoyed a second furlough. The family had just learned that Mrs. Luikens was pregnant once more. On the return trip, shortly after embarking from Rotterdam, a momentous event took place.

> *FF: On the way back - one day away from The Netherlands - I was born on the ship, the SS KAWI* [registered in The Netherlands].
>
> *EF: She was born in the Bay of Biscay, west of France.*
>
> *MFG:* [remembering a family anecdote] *And the captain wrote a book?*
>
> *FF: Well, the captain said how do you call your baby, and my mam* [mom] *said she hadn't made up her mind. The captain said why don't you call her Kawina, after the ship KAWI? There is a book called Kawina, but it has nothing to do with me.*

Despite the captain's fanciful suggestion, the parents named the infant Frederika Adriana Luikens, born November 18, 1916.

The next month the SS KAWI arrived in the port of Padang, Sumatra.

FF: My birth was registered in Padang, as this was the first city we encountered with a Dutch birth registry.

Back aboard, the family went on to Batavia, the KAWI's final destination. By another vessel they returned to their home in Palembang.

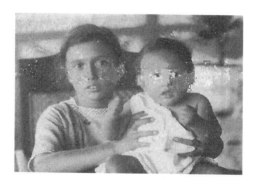

Ten-year-old Marie with infant Rika

******

By this time the Flissingers had moved once more, back to Batavia. Certainly devastated by the loss of their two young daughters, they nonetheless continued their pursuit to have a family. The results were gratifying. On

September 16, 1916, Willem (Willie) Rudolf Flissinger was born.

The following year, on November 9, 1917, Ernest Huibert (spelled Hubert in later years) Flissinger entered the world.

4.

SIX POUND WEAKLING

Nes always delighted in the memories of his childhood, even though he had it tough in the beginning.

> *EF: I was only six pounds at birth and very frail. The doctor said, "That boy's never going to make it." I was constantly in hospitals. For months at a stretch I got injections for this or that sickness.*
>
> Because I was so frail I had lots of nicknames, such as "peking", a very small bird. My mother called me "miep" because I always heaved and panted for air. And because of that bronchial condition, from our servant, Ne Ne, I got the name "nini". All these names were used by the family at one time or another.

****

Although Frans had an aversion to East Java, he moved his family to various towns back there, probably spurred by promotions. He had become a controller of the post office. And despite the frailty of son number two, the parents didn't hesitate to increase their issue.

In Bangil, East Java came two more sons, René Adolf Flissinger on April 27, 1919, and Bertus (Bert) Cornelis Flissinger on September 1, 1920.

EF: My first recollection of being consciously aware of my parents was in Bangil when I was hiding behind a big tree and my mother found me. She was dressed in a sarong, a native dress, even though she was a Dutch citizen.

**

EF: At that time the isolators for telephones were made with silver. There were little porcelain cups filled with molten silver and those fumes would make me very sick. But the doctors back then couldn't diagnose what it was, so I was in and out of hospitals continually. The doctors said I was not going to live one year and every year it was extended, until seven years. I couldn't play in the rain, couldn't play in the wind. We had an old servant who was a babysitter for my mother. She was very strict and when I got out in the rain she'd say, "I'm going to tell Pappy [Poppy]." That was bad, because Pap [Pop] always had his horsewhip ready. Sometimes she said, "I tell your mother." That was all right. I wasn't afraid of my mother.

**

At age four, as a surprise from my pap, I got a baby monkey. It was a black loetoeng with a very long tail and a lighter-colored nose. I named him Jacob, and Jacob became a friend.

I want to emphasize the happy childhood I had with Jacob and a sheep and a stray dog. Even though I could not play - roughhouse - with my brothers, I still had my three animals and they were my friends.

There was a huge tree in our yard with a real wide base. There were holes between the exposed roots and I let my imagination run free. I thought of little dwarfs dressed in beautiful clothes and all with tall caps. These were also my friends. I built them a house. I wanted my younger brothers, René and Bert, to join me, but they would tease me about my dreams. Yet I loved my brothers. Until I could play with them, I was on my own.

Our large yard - about two acres - was surrounded by plastered cement walls six feet high. The plaster was peeling off at several places. One day I pulled off a large piece of plaster and I felt a painful sting in my right hand. It turned out to be a scorpion that took my fingers for a prey. I was real ill for a few days.

Not the whole yard was kept up. The back part had tall grass. There I found snakes and turtles and lizards and other kinds of animals. Snakes fascinated me and I played with them from early childhood. Luckily, I was never bitten by a poisonous snake.

I love fruit and we had lots of fruit trees in our yard. To name a few: mangos, bananas, zuurzak, djamboe, klobok and djamboeaer, and even durian (which I did not like until I was much older.) The fruit is the size of a basketball, has lots of stickers or thorns, and smells terrible. The smell - or better yet, the odor - stayed with you for a long time after you ate them. Because I loved fruit, I soon got the nickname of Tjodot (fruit bat). I never saw anything in it to pick a fruit from the ground or out of the creek running through our yard and consume it with pleasure.

Jacob was a lovable, misunderstood animal - and full of mischief. When he was a baby he was bottle-fed, but it did not take long before he ate fresh fruits. When he was able to move around he was taken out of his cage and got a collar around his middle which was attached to a long chain fastened to a steel pole about ten feet high. On top of the pole a little "house" was built, an open cage with a little porch. About 4:00 p.m. every afternoon my father gave Jacob a hot bun to eat and he loved it. He took the bun to his porch, ate until he had enough, and then crumpled the rest and dripped the crumbs at the base of the post. At that same time of day my mother released the chickens and ducks, and there were a whole lot. They knew where to get a treat and traveled to Jacob's "place" where they started pecking at the crumbs. Jacob was watching and he always had the one with the most feathers in mind. If it was close enough Jacob threw himself on it, held it between his feet, and started plucking the poor thing! The ruckus that followed - lots of cackling - was deafening! Then everybody came out of the house to rescue the victim. Pap would give Jacob a good thrashing with a cane and Jacob would release the fowl. This did not prevent Jacob from doing this over and over again, day after day.

Why my father did not stop giving him a bun every afternoon is beyond me. Maybe Pap liked to see all those plucked, naked chickens trot around our big yard.

Each afternoon, after the "chicken pluck", I took Jacob out for a walk. I always dressed him up in baby clothes that my mother gave me. Jacob sat on my shoulder and had his fingers in my hair. I fed him peanuts which I had to put in his mouth after taking the shells off. If I was too slow he let me know by giving my hair a good jerk, which hurt, and he would scream until he had his nuts.

Jacob grew to be about thirty inches tall, sitting, and about twenty-five pounds, and he had long arms. He was very smart. Many a time he broke away from his chain and had to be retrieved. One day a neighbor called to tell us that our Jacob was on the man's chandelier with his chain tangled in the crystal ornaments. Another time Jacob was in someone's pantry. Once Jacob was heard crying his lungs out at the top of a huge, fifty-foot kapoek tree. His chain was entwined in the thin branches. Nobody could reach him so the whole tree had to come down.

On another occasion, when we were walking in a park, Jacob got away from me and started to push a baby buggy with a baby in it. He had wrestled the buggy from the baby's mother. She was very angry with me. I apologized, but she called my pap and I was grounded for a month.

Jacob may have been a tyrant to others, but he was an amusement and a blessing to me.

5.

THE LORD TAKETH AWAY

In early 1922 the Luikenses were preparing to furlough a third time to The Netherlands. Johannes was by then a vice-president with Royal Dutch Shell. But the trip was not to be.

> *FF: My father got a heart attack and died on January 8, 1922* [at the Pladjoe oil refinery in Palembang, Sumatra]. *He was fifty-six.*

Marie, Rika's mother, was pregnant with her seventh child.

> *FF: After my father died – four days later my younger brother, Jantje, died. He was born premature on January 11, and lived less than a day* [died January 12]. *My father and brother were buried next to each other.*

> *EF: Riek was the youngest of the nest. She lost her father when she was 5 years old, but remarkably she remembers many things about him. She remembers him lying on his death bed and she was stroking his feet to rid them of some ants that she saw. She did not realize why her pappy was sleeping.*

There is another memory that has stayed with Frederika

through the years. Many nights, as the children were put to bed, Johannes would move from bedside to bedside, hands clasped behind his back, reciting this prayer:

De dag is weer gedaald.
    The day is done.
De nacht is weer voorhanden.
    The night is at hand.
Heer Jezus blijft ons bij.
    Lord Jesus, be with us.
Hoedt ons voor zonde en schande.
    Protect us against sin and shame.
Wijst ons de rechte weg, en
    Show us the right way, and
Open ons gezicht, en
    Give us insight, and
Toon ons, Lieve God, hiernamaals,
    Show us, Dear God, hereafter,
Het Eeuwig Licht.
    The Eternal Light.

Gij zult uw ouders nederig eren
    Thou shalt humbly honor thy parents
Opdat uw God, die eeuwig leeft,
    So that God, who is eternal,
Hun dagen gunstig moogt vermeerderen
    May increase their lifespan
In het land waar Zijne hand u heeft
    In the land where He keeps you.

Following Johannes's passing Marie made it a point to

teach the prayer to her children. [Frederika would find comfort in it throughout her life, remembering her father, and she, in turn, taught the prayer to her own children. Her daughter, Marguerite, inspired by the prayer's family history, thought it most certainly should be included herein and prays this prayer to this day.]

As was her nature, Marie displayed concern for those other than herself. She was aware of the impact Johannes's death would have on little Rika. She gave her daughter a locket inside which was a picture of Johannes. Rika would be able to wear the locket around her neck, keeping her father close to her heart.

****

On March 8, 1922, in Den Helder, The Netherlands, Franciscus Jacobus de la Fonteyne, Rika's great-grandfather, passed away at the age of ninety-one.

****

FF: After my father died, my mother and all of us children went to Batavia where Opa Franciscus, my grandfather from my mother's side, lived. He had worked in the military but by that time he was already retired. He took care of us for about a year.

MG: When your father passed away, you were just starting school probably.

FF: Yes, when I was six I went into the first grade in Batavia at the Catholic school with the nuns, the Sisters Ursulinen Klooster [cloister].

MFG: Was that a girls' school?

FF: Yes.

MG: What were the ages of the girls?

FF: That was a grammar school, a high school, and a teachers education school, all right there.

MG: And your sister, Moes, was already there?

FF: She and my sister, Marie, were already boarded there when we were still in Palembang, because in Palembang there was no high school.

** **

FF: After about a year with my grandfather my mother bought a home on Struiswykstraat, #11. She bought that house with the money that the Shell Company had given her as a pension - a one-time deal because of my father's passing. It was a real beautiful house. It also had a flower shop annexed to it. Mam ran the shop for about a year but had to stop the business because she developed a rash from the flowers.

MG: Were there other aunts and uncles?

FF: My mother had two sisters and two brothers.

MG: Were they around you?

FF: Not much. They came to visit us once in a while, but we did not have much to do with them.

MG: Of your siblings, who were you closest to?

FF: Mostly Jopie. She was only three years older.

MG: So you went to the same schools?

FF: Yes, we all went through that Catholic school. Except my brother. He went to a government school and then a five year college.

MG: Did you and Jopie have activities outside school?

FF: Yes, we both played korfball [a mixed-gender team sport involving a ball and a hoop or basket].

MG: How would you characterize your relationship with Moes?

FF: It was good.

MG: Did you have activities with her?

FF: No, not much. She was so much older.

MG: And the next in line was Marie. Was it different with her?

FF: No, she was closer to Moes than to me when we were young, but we were closer when we were adults.

MG: How close were you with your brother?

FF: Oh, my brother was pretty good. We were nice together. Well, we fought once in a while, but he was good. I found a little broken statue on the side of the house when we moved in - it was a little Catholic statue of Mother Mary and Child. He took it and fixed it. I still have the statue.

MG: What was your relationship with Fietje?

FF: Oh, Fietje was five years older.

MG: Did you do things with her?

FF: She went walking with me once in a while.

MG: What was the day-to-day interaction with your mother when you were young?

FF: She was a good mother and we were always around her. And we went to the movies with her on Saturdays.

MG: What type of film was playing?

FF: Uh, with the five little kids...

MFG: "The Little Rascals"?

FF: Yes.

MG: Now, your mom didn't do the cooking because you had...

FF: We had maids, but she was the one that told them what to do.

MG: Did you learn cooking from your mother?

FF: Not really. I saw often how the maids did it. That's the way I remembered. And what I didn't know I asked questions how to do it.

****

On August 22, 1923, Franciscus Antonius Everhard de la Fonteyne passed away at age sixty-seven in Batavia.

FF: I only really knew Opa Franciscus for that one year we lived with him. He used to take me places once in a while. I remember he was a nice man.

6.

SPOILED ROTTEN

Sometime around 1923 Frans Flissinger's employment took him and his family to the city of Djombang in East Java.

EF: Upon growing older whatever sickness I had did not go away, and one time I heard a doctor say to my mom, "He might make it to be seven years old." This did not mean much to me and actually it did not make an impression on me. But around age five I noticed that I was kept away from playing in the rain with my younger brothers, René and Bert.

With all the attention I got because I was sickly I became a brat. I was always whining and it must have upset my parents very much. My older brother, Willie, was very tolerant. So was Bert, more easy-going. But René? No way. René couldn't stand it that I was so spoiled. And I was. I always wanted to have my way. René did not like the idea and wanted it the way he saw it. The inevitable result was that René and I were always fighting. Finally my pap got tired of it. He was controller of the post office and the post office was an annex to our house with access from the house. In the post office was a soundproof room with metal doors like a vault. Well, one day our fighting got so bad that my father locked René and me in that big soundproof room and said, "Fight it out." The door was closed and we went at it. Before too long my pap opened the door. It was obvious that René had gotten the better of me. Pap couldn't stop laughing about it. We did not fight anymore after that.

**

At age six I started school. The school years were uneventful. I do remember that I wanted to have a cow real bad. Across from the school and not far from our house was a large soccer field on which a dairy company had the milk cows grazing. I picked out the cow I wanted. She had a rope around the neck. I grabbed the rope and started walking homeward. After a few minutes I looked back and noticed that all the milk cows were following. I did not know that I had chosen the lead cow!

Also when I was about six years old I was allowed to play with my brothers. René, Bert, and I became "The Three Musketeers". I was the oldest but I was the smallest and weakest. René was definitely the leader. We were always in trouble due to our mischievousness. I especially enjoyed the games we played in the pouring rain. And Djombang is where I learned to ride a bike. One of the postmen taught me. It was fun.

All the water we consumed had to be boiled in huge drums to get rid of bacteria that might cause illnesses. There was a lid on these drums.

The boiling of the water was closely supervised by my mother. The water could only be taken out of the barrel if the water had really boiled for some time on the wood fire. One day my mother said, "Miep, check and see if the water is boiling." René heard this and we ran to the drums. Because René was faster and healthier he got there first and lifted the lid. For some reason I stuck my whole right arm in the boiling water! No real harm, but I really screamed. My pap was not pleased that I had done such a foolish thing.

** **

In Djombang, on November 20, 1924, Frans and Martina gave birth to a fifth son, Jacobus (Ko, for short) Martinus Flissinger.

** **

Besides my monkey, a sheep, a big dog, and other animals, I had some birds, turtles, lizards, and other kinds of animals found in the yard. And as I mentioned we had all kinds of fruit trees.

In the big, two-acre yard there were lots of flower pots on pedestals on the left front side with roses in them. Good hiding places. Along the entrance to the yard was a Chinese grocery store. It was my parents' main supplier. The owner gave us plenty of candy for free.

In front of our house was a railroad track and a long train came by two or three times a day, announcing its approach with loud whistles. The tracks and streets were lined with huge kanari trees and lots of squirrels lived in them. One squirrel fell on the street and was dazed. I felt sorry for it and picked it up. But the squirrel did not appreciate it and put its teeth all the way through my left middle finger. I did not tell my mam or pap about it, which was very dangerous.

Every afternoon after school the three musketeers had to take a nap with Pap in a huge bed. After we thought Pap was asleep we tried to slip out. Many times we got caught and the order, "Get back!" was enough to keep us in bed till about 4:00 p.m. After the nap we had tea and snacks. This always was a treat to me.

7.

RELIGIOUS FERVOR

Just a couple weeks shy of her twenty-second birthday Albertine Hermanna (Moes) Luikens, on June 22, 1927, became an apprentice nun with the Sisters Ursulinen Klooster in Batavia. Two years later she took the holy vows. She chose to be called Sister Alexia in respect for her mother who was sadly missing her own brother, Alex, whose whereabouts were unknown at the time.

****

FF: When I was about ten, I went to board at the Ursulinen Klooster. I was in the fifth grade. I boarded there for about five years.

MG: How close was that to where you lived?

FF: It was in the same city and I could go home every weekend.

MFG: Why did you board there?

FF: Moes was there and thought it would be better if I stayed there.

8.

BOYS WILL BE BOYS

No matter where the Flissinger family resided, there were always ways for youngsters to be fascinated and entertained - and get into trouble.

In the year 1926 we moved to Bandung in West Java. Here our life and routine was much like Djombang. Then in 1927 we lived in Djocja in the southern part of Middle Java for about six months. It was a pleasant town and we lived in a house on a street called Bintarang Tengah. It was a big house. Here we had lots of fun. René, naturally, was the leader. When we were supposed to take a nap in the afternoon (we did not take a nap with our pap anymore), we went to a river that was close to the house. The river was full of "bloodsuckers". They look like little fish in the water, but if you stepped in the water they attacked warm-blooded animals instead of swimming away like fish. We always got a few on our legs no matter how fast we jumped through the water. Then came the job of plucking them off. We had cigarettes with us for this purpose, got one wet, and put the tobacco juice on the slimy creatures which then dropped off instantly. After about a half hour we went home knowing full well that Pap was waiting at the door with his trusty stick. We all got it real good. Then, in our room we counted the number of bloodsucker stripes on our legs and rear ends to see who had "won".

**

Pap and Mam and Ko moved again to Bandung. The constant moving from town to town took a toll on our schooling, so this time Willie, René, Bert, and I had to stay in Djocja and were boarded with a friend of Pap we called Oom [uncle].

Oom's house was real big and was connected to a conference room for the Masons. Our bedroom was right next to the conference room. All of us slept in a very big bed with steel posts at the corners and mosquito netting over the bed. We did not know it but one night there was a big Masons meeting.

To go out from our room we had to go through Oom's bedroom. In there was lots of hair oil (cream). René had hair that stood up like spikes. That night he decided to flatten his hair so it would stick to his head. He used Oom's cream. It was always hot in Indie and René smelled like a barber shop! Grease dripped from his face and the back of his head.

Then hell broke loose. René put his hand through his dripping hair. With the dirty hand he tried to touch each of us and ran after us. We jumped on and off the bed, through the mosquito netting, and made lots of noise! This ended abruptly when the Masons meeting was

38

interrupted and Oom came in the room and saw the trouble and damage. When confronted by Oom, René could not deny using the cream.

**

Oom was fond of his chickens. His instructions were that nobody could collect his chicken eggs but himself. Well, one time in the afternoon during nap time René, Bert, and I collected the eggs. We gave them to Oom's wife and then climbed a big tree and sat in the top until Oom came out in a rage. We pretended not to be able to get down, afraid we would fall. After we got down we got a punishment anyway.

We were there with Oom about three months till school was finished and he put us on a train to Bandung. None too soon for Oom, I imagine.

**

A German doctor told Pap that he should try something else to cure me of whatever I had instead of sending me to doctors and hospitals with no results. The ages I was predicted to live to were five, seven, ten, and eleven. Well, I was already eleven and alive, but not healthy. This doctor told Pap to have me lay in the sun on the roof of our house for an hour a day - naked - half an hour on my back and half an hour on my tummy. I did this sun treatment for six months and it seemed to cure me for good from whatever I had. I never have been sick again with the same symptoms. There were broken bones and other diseases, but those came later. Naturally school was missed, about two hours a day, but there was a priest who was willing to help me and I stayed two to three hours after school.

9.

BRANCHING OUT

Around 1927 Marie Luikens, then twenty, encountered a young man named Willem van der Torren (born with surname Benjamin but adopted by a Mr. van der Torren). The Luikens family tree was about to sprout another limb.

> *MG: Do you remember how your sister and Willem met?*
>
> *FF: I think they met at church. Mr. van der Torren, Willem's father, lived in Sumatra but sent Willem to live in Java, in an orphanage.*
>
> *MG: When did they marry?*
>
> *FF: Around 1928, I believe.*
>
> *MG: Where did they live?*
>
> *FF: When they got married Willem was working in Sumatra, so Marie went there too. That was in Padang, in north Sumatra.*

But Cupid wasn't finished shooting his arrows at these two families. Rika's brother, Wolter, met Willem's adoptive sister, also named Marie (van der Torren, legitimate daughter of Mr. van der Torren), born October 24, 1909, in Sawahlunto, Sumatra. Wolter and Marie soon established an enduring relationship.

10.

THE MOTHERLAND

On June 6, 1929, the Flissingers had one more son, Martinus (Tinus, for short) Jacobus Flissinger, born in Bandung. Soon after his birth the whole family, plus a nanny, went to The Netherlands on Frans's earned furlough.

> *EF: I was eleven years old when we arrived in Holland and settled in The Hague. Instead of the typical eight months, we stayed in Holland about a year and a half because Pap was ill for a while. We met some relatives who were also on furlough and some who had never left Holland.*

The Dutch called us colonists, but as a whole they did not know what colonies were or where they were located. They were well aware that the Indies produced lots of money for their coffers, but how the money was earned was a mystery.

They also thought that we did not live in houses with marble floors. They thought our floors were made of clay. Whatever we told them they could not seem to comprehend.

There was discrimination against us. We children did not know what that was all about because we were buddies with the natives in Indonesia and did not notice any strange attitudes or treatments. I did not pay much attention to it there in Holland but I noticed that Pap was bothered. He had a big, long mustache and was asked many a time if he was with the circus. His answer was always, "Je gekke moeder is met de circus! (Your crazy mother is with the circus!)" Mam did not experience the discrimination because she was born in Delft and was fair complected.

We went to school in Holland and found that we were far ahead in our studies and that our universities were better. Many Dutch thought that we did not have school in Indie.

The schooling was fairly uneventful but fun. All the students had to take a bath weekly and were taken to a "bath house" where big Dutch women were on duty. They saw to it that the children were properly soaped and scrubbed. I usually got an extra turn because they wanted me "clean" - that is, they wanted my brown neck to be lighter.

We kids did not develop lasting relationships with so-called "friends". René, Bert, and I were always together and that was enough for us. Even though I was still a weakling, I was allowed to keep company with my two brothers. And the three musketeers always got in trouble. René, our leader, developed his full potential. We had a great time, though the punishments were often severe.

As we were ahead at school we had it easy with lots of free time on our hands. This time was mostly spent in the duinen (dunes) close to the ocean and at the grachten (canals). In the dunes we saw many couples being very "cozy", but we were not really interested in that kind of thing until years later.

I did lots of fishing in the canals and at the North Sea. One of my favorite spots in the canals was in Loos duinen, close to the vegetable market, and in Scheveningen at the ocean. I did quite a bit of fishing in Scheveningen. In winter, however, it could be very cold - so cold that my fingers were too stiff to put the bait on the hook - so I joined René and Bert skating on the frozen canals. In summer these canals were our swimming pools. (I would not swim in them now. I saw the canals many years later and they were very dirty.)

In fall and winter of 1929, during The Depression, we saw boatloads of vegetables and milk and milk products being destroyed or plowed under. We did not understand why. We were told that the goods could not be sold for too low a price. I thought it was shameful.

I took piano lessons for about a year. I lacked musical talents but I could play a tune, which gave my father the idea that I could accompany him while he was playing his flute. But Pap was very impatient. If I made a mistake twice, he would get very upset and the musical harmony was stopped until the next time. Finally it was stopped altogether and I lost interest.

11.

PATERNAL INSTINCT

The widowed Mrs. Luikens had a lot on her plate managing a large house and servants and raising six children alone. There was a time, though, that she had a bit of help.

Rika's father had a very good friend, a tall man with a very distinguished appearance named Klaas Decker. After Johannes's passing, Opa Decker, as he was respectfully called, thought it his duty, even though he and Mam Luikens were not very close, to look after the family of his friend.

MG: How did he get involved with your family?

FF: Opa Decker worked with my father in Palembang, Sumatra, and he was his best friend. And when my father passed away, Opa kept in contact with my mother and the children. But he was still working in Sumatra. We were in Java. Then quite a bit later he retired and he went back and forth to The Netherlands. But when he was in Java he stayed on our property in a separate house.

MG: How old were you when he first came to live with you?

FF: I'm not sure, but I think I was about thirteen or fourteen.

MJG: Was he married? Did he have any children?

FF: He was not married, but he had a daughter. I think she was born from an Indonesian woman that he had as a caretaker. Opa raised the girl and took her as a daughter to Holland and that was where she lived the rest of her life.

MG: And he felt some sort of obligation to watch out for your family?

FF: Yes.

MG: How was your relationship with him?

FF: I remember he was very strict with us children.

✶✶✶✶

On June 15, 1930, Willem and Marie van der Torren bore their first child, Sonja van der Torren, in Padang, Sumatra.

Willem, for what appears to be defiance, refused to allow Marie to give their daughter a middle name. It was customary in those days that a middle name would be chosen to respectfully honor a preceding family member or perhaps a religious figure. Apparently Willem would have none of either.

12.

RETURN TO PARADISE

The long vacation was certainly a luxury for Frans and his family, but furloughs are, of course, designed to be temporary.

In early 1931 the whole family went back to the East Indies where my father was going to be stationed in Serang, the capital of West Java. The ship took more than a month to reach Batavia. On board I met a priest, Pastoor Molenaar, who became my friend. He was a brilliant man, spoke or had knowledge of twenty-eight languages, and during the trip he studied Malay. He was to be stationed on a small island, Flores, to the east of Java and north of Australia. When we parted he gave me a rosary, a beaded chain with a cross attached. I had no idea how much it would come to mean to me.

His first stay was in Toda Beleu and after that in Maumere where he worked as a priest, a brother. Then he was on Flores Island until he died at the age of eighty. It was beyond me, and still is, why an eminently smart person is placed in isolation where his talents were wasted. We stayed in contact with each other through the years. Often he asked for a favor - like a bike, a soccer ball, or an air gun. My pap bought him those things and he apparently enjoyed the gifts.

(He never met my wife but in his letters to me he addressed her too. I would like to have had a chance to meet him again.)

**

What a good time we had there in Serang. We went to school – that's where I finished my grammar school – but we had lots of free time. Willie was always doing things by himself and before long he was boarded in Batavia for high school. Ko was still a boy and Tinus, of course, still an infant.

EF: Serang was in the middle of the jungle. There were many Europeans working there and the house we lived in was huge, like all the other houses we occupied in the Indies. Our yard must have been more than an acre, with lots of coconut, mango, papaya, and sawoh trees. My youth was fantastic. We lived up on a pedestal. The Indonesians were just beautiful to us.

FF: Yes, they were very good to us.

**

I liked animals and had a menagerie of them. There were alligators, crocodiles, snakes, lizards, turtles, and all kinds of birds in cages, mainly songbirds that woke me up in the morning, and then geese, ducks, chickens, and even turkeys, goats, and a trenggiling (anteater). All the animals were easy to obtain and I collected all kinds of them. One of my favorites was snakes, big and small, poisonous or non-poisonous, but because my mother was scared of them, I had to get rid of them.

I usually collected the animals during my hunting in the jungles. The anteater I found in a tree. The natives had nailed it by its tail to the tree with a spike. His whiskers and some scales were removed. The natives believed that these things had magical powers. I took this animal home and put him in a cage. His food consisted of termites and eggs and larvae. Native boys got this food for me for one cent a load. I spent about four cents a day. But I could not depend on the native boys so I let the animal go in our yard. We had lots of trees. The first tree the anteater climbed was a coconut tree. After cleaning the crown of ants he rolled himself into a ball and dropped out of the tree with a bounce. This happened for several days and nights until he found his way out of our fenced yard.

There was an abundance of everything - fruit, animals, fish, snakes, etc. Also plentiful were the flying foxes, bat-like animals the size of a small dog with a wingspan of six to seven feet. They smelled somewhat like a skunk. People of some tribes liked to eat them. They knew how to remove the glands. I wanted either to shoot them or catch them. They were easy to tame and train. We had a huge sawoh tree in the yard and that tree had fruit the size of a pear. The fruit tasted good and had a sweet-smelling aroma.

The flying foxes and fruit bats loved them. Here I saw my chance to get some of them. I built a platform almost in the top of the tree, about thirty feet up, and took position at around 7:00 p.m. Soon they came and I could shoot them with my pellet gun from a distance of two feet. I gave these animals to the people who loved to eat them. I caught one alive for my menagerie, but I had to let it go mainly for reasons of the smell that my mam could not stand.

Among my animals there was a funny relationship between my goat and a rooster. The rooster sat all day on the back of the goat. The goat did not seem to mind the hitchhiker.

At an earlier age, I made up my mind that I was going to become a medical doctor. I showed this interest in the treatment of all the animals I had. We had no veterinarian, so when an animal was sick I usually treated it myself. My operating equipment consisted of a sharp knife, spoons, a needle, and sewing thread. I used iodine on all my needles. Remarkably most of my animals survived.

**

In the keuken (kitchen), the bijgebouwen (outbuildings], the gudangs (storerooms), and the servants quarters we had lots of geckoes that crawled up walls and ceilings. So did small lizards (tjitjaks) which laid their eggs in keyholes. They often hid between the door and the door jam and when the door was closed a lizard would be squashed and you could hear it. I had to remove the tjitjaks.

One day we thought we heard noises of lizards behind a large chest where my mother stored all kinds of beverages and fruits on liquor. Upon investigation, it turned out that it was René. He had a bottle of fruit on liquor between his legs and he was taking the fruit out with his fingers, eating the fruit, and smacking louder and louder. He did not know that he could get drunk from the fruit. He seemed to have enjoyed it.

**

We had a huge cabinet where the china and silverware were stored. Also, on the top shelf, were candies and cookies. The cabinet was about nine feet high - and not secured on the backside. In order to get to the goodies I climbed the shelves as if they were stepladder steps. As I got to the top shelf the chest got top-heavy and toppled. It came down with a crash with me under it. All the chinaware broke. After I was cleaned up to see how badly I was hurt, which was not too bad, I was put on restriction for one month. Boy, that was hard.

**

When Willie was about fifteen, he went to a doctor concerning an ailment in his right knee. The doctor diagnosed the problem incorrectly and administered a medication that had an adverse effect. From that point on Willie was a bit impaired physically.

EF: He was broad-shouldered and strong, but he was a very likeable man. He never did anything in sports because his right leg was lame. But Willie was a very strong man. One time I saw him lift a loaded wagon. One wheel had sunk into a hole. He put his shoulders underneath the axle and brought the wheel to ground level and the wagon was pulled out.

**

For René, Bert, and me there was a tendency by then to be away from each other due to different interests, but we still had fun together. Often we went to the cinema where cowboy films were shown. After the shows everybody was a cowboy.

And there was still mischief.

There was a building, annexed to the post office where my father was the boss, which was loaded with beautiful temple birds. They had a blue-gray color with a white neck and a really red beak. They nested in the ceiling of that building. One night René woke Bert and me up about 4:00 a.m. and said, "Let's catch temple birds." Well, we armed ourselves with flashlights and went in the ceiling. The light of the flashlight shone in their eyes and they could not move. It was good picking, like fruit from a tree. I was the one to receive them after being caught. I put the birds in my shirt. So did Bert. But these birds could bite with their short beaks. Our shirts got fuller and fuller and the birds scratched and bit our bellies and backs. It was ticklish also. We laughed and stumbled around. Suddenly I smelled something rotten under my nose. René was laughing uncontrollably. He had found rotten birds eggs and thought it was fun to share the stench. It did not take long for Bert and me to find more rotten eggs. René got most of them in his hair and face. Then suddenly we heard the stern call of my pap to come down from the ceiling. He saw our shirts and heard the noise under them. He ordered us to release the birds.

**

Alongside the post office was a church with a high steeple. The church smelled like bats and there were thousands and thousands of them. At dusk they came out and early in the morning they came back. You could not see them fly in. They dropped from a good height and the breaking of the drop close to the roosting place made a "furring" sound. And with the thousands of incoming bats it sounded strange and eerie.

The church was separated from the post office by a stone wall. We used it as front row seating to listen to a band that played on Saturdays in the nearby soos (club).

**

Through our yard ran a little creek, not wider than two feet, that was loaded with fish and I caught lots of them and gave them to the servants. They loved to eat them and we did not care for them. Some catfish were almost three feet long. I wondered how they could live in that narrow ditch.

One day in this same creek I saw a snake head coming out of the water. As soon as it saw me, it vanished. I laid in wait with a rake. When he came up again, I swung the rake and hooked him behind the head. It was a beautiful water snake about eight feet long and very big around the middle. He had lots of fish in him.

**

There was a lake called Tassi Cardie about ten kilometers from Serang. We liked to swim in that lake even though it had lots of crocks and electric eels in it. We were lucky. The jolt of electricity an eel releases is real big. One of our acquaintances was killed that way in another lake. He drowned.

Also at the lake was a tree that was a gathering place, in mating season, for black and white snakes - poisonous. They were six to seven feet long. Hundreds of them. They were good for target practice.

**

I fished and hunted to my heart's content. The Java Sea and the dammed fishponds (empangs) were stocked with ocean fish. There was no trouble to find game of any kind.

The natives were very friendly and whenever I came to hunt I was treated to lunch or dinner in the native huts.

FF: They did that for anybody that came through their villages.

EF: When I was hungry, I could shoot any coconut from the tree and eat it. And if I shot squirrels or flying foxes - kalongs (bats) - the natives rewarded me with all kinds of fruits that those animals ate.

At first I had a 4.5 mm pellet gun and my first animals were wild doves, like the mourning dove and the green doves. The latter loved the little figs that came on the banyan trees almost all year. The birds would flock to the huge trees. All I had to do was lie on my back and shoot the birds with my pellet gun. After I had six or seven birds, I went home and asked the cook to prepare them for me.

I did quite a bit of hunting, not just with the pellet gun I had but with a 16-gauge shotgun. The gun was even taller than I was. Even though I was not sickly anymore I had not grown much. At the age of thirteen I was not taller than 4 feet.

One time I was allowed to go hunting with the big people. We were going for wild boar and tiger. I was given a 16-gauge double barrel gun and some shells with large lead pellets. Mr. Schrijn stationed me in the fork of a big tree and told me to look for tiger. If one came, it would attack a water buffalo calf that was tied down in a clearing. Before I knew it a tiger appeared, took the calf, and disappeared with me never firing a shot. Naturally I was ridiculed. But if I had fired I probably would have been blown out of the tree, because later that day we went boar hunting and I had another chance to use the 16-guage. There was this big stork in the swamp. I aimed, pulled the trigger, got a big kick in my right shoulder, and lay in the mud with my hands, arms, and legs up in the air. But when I got up I saw that I got the stork! I got laughed at but was also praised. It felt great and I felt like a big man at thirteen years old.

I loved the jungle and hunting there. René occasionally accompanied me. In a swamp close to the sea, fish were cultivated, very large and very good to eat. This place was also a resting place for migrating birds. The biggest group was ducks. René had a rifle and I had a double barrel shotgun. The swamp was also inhabited by large and small alligators. Well, I shot a duck and it landed some distance away and I started to retrieve it, waist-deep in the water. Suddenly I heard René scream, "Ernest, duck!" Now, with René, you cannot be sure. If he says something, you have to watch out, is it a joke or not.

MFG: So he was a big joker.

EF: Yes, a big joker. But I went down under the water anyway. Then I heard a "thud" on top of the water.

MFG: So he wasn't kidding.

EF: No, he was not. I said, "What did you shoot at?"

He said, "Look at that." A six foot crocodile had approached me from the back and René saw it and killed it with one shot. That was all the hunting we did for that day.

13.

TROPICAL TRAUMAS

The equatorial regions, with extreme heat and humidity, are notorious for debilitating diseases. Java was no exception.

Mosquitoes were there by the millions. If you slapped a person on the back, your hand left a bloody hand print from all the mosquitoes that were killed. Malaria was always a possibility. One time my pap said, "Take these." They were quinine pills. Within an hour I was itching all over and my whole body was swollen. We did not know what it was from. Well, the doctor came and after some investigating he concluded that I was allergic to quinine. He was sure it was the problem and to prevent malaria I had to take atropine pills. I got malaria anyway.

**

Once I was hunting by myself in the jungle. I got thirsty and hungry. It did not take long to find a coconut tree. I climbed the tree and got myself a nice young coconut. I cut the coconut, drank the water, and then split the fruit. Instead of making myself a scoop out of the coconut husk, I went to a stream close by and found a shell, rinsed it off, and enjoyed the sweet young coconut. A few days later I got a high temperature. I had typhoid fever. It was very severe and I was in a coma for many days. I was not in the hospital but was treated at home. The doctor, an older gentleman, came to visit me sometimes twice a day. I could hear his car speeding up the yard and breaking like a maniac. I got over the disease in month and a half, but a few weeks later I had a relapse. I was in bed for three and a half months. Then I had to be on a strict diet and all my hair was shaved off. I was as bald as a billiard ball for at least six months. While I was very sick I remember "floating" all over the bed looking for my rosary, the one Father Molenaar had given me. I finally found it and fell asleep for many, many hours. I was told later that I was in a coma.

**

A short time after my bout with typhoid fever, I got in an argument with Willie over my pellet gun. I was lounging under a palm tree and for one reason or another we had a fight. My father came out, took the gun, and hit it on the ground and the tree. It was bent in all kinds of shape. Kaput. Willie felt so sorry that he worked on the gun, straightened it out, and I could shoot with it as before. The only thing missing was the sight, but that did not bother me.

**

After I got well enough to be active outside again I played soccer with my brothers in the park across from our house. It was a rainy day and the field was soggy. I fell, slid for a distance, and my left arm got caught in a hole. I broke my left arm in two places below the elbow. The weeks and months that followed, visiting the doctor, were a nightmare. For some reason the bones would not heal properly. My arm had to be re-broken and reset - seven times! And there was no anesthesia! I was tied down in a chair and two male nurses pulled on my arm in opposite directions while the doctor put on a splint. The pain was terrible. All I could do was scream and cry. Finally, when the seventh cast was taken off it was decided that we could try to let it heal by itself. I was so glad that my arm did not have to be set again. But even after it was reasonably healed it was still crooked and a bone was sticking out under the skin at the wrist. Pap sent me to a specialist in Batavia. This doctor gave me two treatments to choose from. One, an operation. Or two, go swimming. I dreaded the thought of another torture so I chose swimming. I'm so glad I did.

14.

PUT TO THE TEST

Education was always a priority in the Flissinger household, and Nes was never lacking in interest or effort.

With all my injury and illness troubles I missed quite a bit of school. I was still very small of stature, self-conscious, and insecure, and I always thought people were laughing at me and ridiculing me. And though I did not realize it at the time, I must have been very nervous.

For me, school was uneventful. I was a good student, learned fast, and did well at class. However, I developed a huge – actually, to me it was <u>tremendously</u> huge – fear of exams. I was very afraid of any test. And even though I was good at all the subjects, I did very poorly on semester finals. I would learn later what my problem was.

**

For some reason Pap didn't want to take care of Ko when it came to his schooling. Ko was about seven years younger than I was and one time - I was only fifteen - Pap said to me, "You take care of Ko. You go to his schools, you go to his teachers, I cannot handle it anymore." My mother was not capable of doing it, so I actually managed Ko's schooling for three years.

**

It was decided that I, like Willie, would board in Batavia for high school. But before that happened, Willie experienced a strange thing at his residence there. One night a knock came at his door. He opened it and there stood a man dressed in black with a high top hat. Willie could not recognize the man's face, but the voice was loud and clear. The man told Willie that Pap was in town (in Serang) for a meeting and that Willie should warn his parents that there was great danger for one of our brothers. Willie immediately phoned home and told of the apparition. We were at a party and were called home and could not go out. Willie rushed home. The next day a policeman was shooting at dogs to prevent the spread of rabies. The gun jammed and Willie tried to help. While Willie had the gun in his hands it went off and the bullet passed between René's legs, very close to his private parts. Fortunately no harm done, but everyone felt this event was pretty eerie.

**

Before I left Serang for good I went hunting one more time with friends. There was a big group of monkeys and I took aim at a big female. She fell. When I came close I could see she was clutching her baby in her arms. She looked up at me with what seemed like tears, as if she were crying. Well, I cried and cried and sobbed. I was so sorry I had done that. I told the other guys that if they did this same thing in my presence, they'd have to deal with me. But it was too late for the female monkey. Even today I am sorry that I could ever have done such a stupid thing. So sorry.

15.

CAPITAL GAINS

Frans was savvy enough to know that his boys would be better off finishing their education in Java's biggest city and capital, Batavia. He sent Nes to follow in Willie's footsteps.

In 1932, while my parents stayed in Serang with my younger brothers, I left for Batavia and was boarded with the same family that Willie was. The oldest son of that family was studying to become a doctor. He was kind of funny. The youngest son, Boet, was building a sailboat. When it was finished it was beautiful. He used it many a time on the river that ran through Batavia. Boet became a friend to me.

EF: And I want to tell something about my older brother, Willie. He was a very smart man. He had a photographic mind. High schools have five years of learning, and after Willie's third year of passing he said to my father, "I quit." It was a very big disappointment to my father because he wanted his children to finish high school.

He asked Willie, "What in the hell do you want to do then?"

Willie said, "I want to go mechanical."

But Pap did not allow the switch. Then one

day a good friend of Pap happened by, heard the story, and convinced Pap that he should allow Willie to do his thing. "Give the boy what he wants, because he's not going to do what you want."

So Willie went to the KWS, a kind of college for engineering, to become a marine machinist. It was a five-year course and Willie had to start from the beginning. But he finished the course in three years and passed the final test magna cum laude. Even a year before he graduated the Marine, Navy, and other organizations tried to lure Willie to their side with all kinds of incentives. He ended up choosing the Navy.

✳✳✳✳✳✳

Willem and Marie van der Torren, still in Padang, Sumatra, welcomed their second child, Roeland (Boetie) van der Torren, on June 18, 1932. (Willem's vehemence regarding middle names came into play again.)

But Willem proved to be an unfaithful husband. Marie, pregnant again, moved back with her two children to Batavia and lived once more with her mother. Divorce was not sanctioned by the Catholic Church so Marie remained a married woman.

On July 31, 1933, there in Batavia, Marie gave birth to her third child, Wolter Franciscus van der Torren. As Willem was no longer a presence in the lives of Marie and her children, Marie did not hesitate to give young Wolter a middle name.

Roeland's nickname, Boetie, came about because his brother, Wolter, when very young, could not pronounce properly the Dutch word for brother, which is broertje.

******

It was lucky I had to go to school in Batavia because there were no organized swim clubs in Serang. I became a member of Tjikini Swim Club. Soon I perfected my swimming, but I really excelled in high dive. I was determined to excel in anything I did.

Swimming did me so much good, both mentally and physically. I grew more than a foot in six months! And when I went home for vacation, still skinny but taller, my parents could hardly recognize me! I felt big mentally too. Needless to say I kept on swimming. I enrolled in swimming as a sport - in particular, high dive. In the meantime I also did gymnastics, boxing, and judo, and performed very well in all those sports.

**

My life's aim was still to become a medical doctor. I did very well at school. I tutored students at high school in mathematics, algebra, planimetrics, physics, etc. When I was at home I was helped by Pap in my languages such as English, French, and German. But I was still insecure and nervous when it came to examinations. When I had to do a test, my mind went blank. All the students I tutored passed, while I turned in blank papers. After an exam I could even tell the other students whether their answers were right or wrong. I went to doctors to try to correct this problem. I was put on a bromide treatment for six months before an exam and it still did not work. Then at last I realized what my problem was. Despite the results of my sporting competitions in which I usually came out on top, I did not believe in myself. It was _me_ that was getting in my way. Finally, with a lot of mental effort, I was able to convince myself that I was going to make it and I came out of exams with flying colors.

But I did not want to go to medical school anymore. Instead I decided to concentrate on becoming a police officer.

16.

UNEXPECTED CHANGE

In 1932 Sister Alexia, Rika's sister, Moes, was sent by the Ursulinen Klooster to the seminary of St. Xaverius in Halfveg, The Netherlands to further her education. In the subsequent four years she achieved a teaching degree in geography, English, and Bahasa Indonesia (the Indonesian language).

******

Like many other countries at that time the East Indies was suffering from economic woes. Among other measures taken, the Dutch government decided that older employees would have to make room for the younger generation. As a result, Frans Flissinger was forced to retire at age forty-five, because by then, 1933, he had twenty-five years with the post office.

> *EF: So our whole family relocated to Batavia. We moved into a house at #13 Struiswykstraat. Next door, in #11, was a family with five girls and one boy. I did not get to know the family at that time, but three years later I would meet my future wife, the youngest member of that family.*

Frans and Martina's 25th wedding anniversary, 1934. Children (clockwise, from left): Ko, René, Willie, Nes, Bert, and Tinus.

17.

SPORTING LIFE

Conditions remained sweet as the Flissingers enjoyed the pleasures of life in the big city. It was especially invigorating for the teenagers.

> We had a motorcycle back then. One day my friend Boet met René. René showed him the motorcycle and Boet said, "I like to drive on these things and I like to ride fast."
>
> René's response was, "Would you like to ride on the back with me?"
>
> "Sure thing," Boet said. So they got on a wide street and René sped up and then he stood up on the motorcycle and spread his arms! When they came back, Boet had to be helped off the bike. He was as pale as a sheet. He never rode with René again.

**

> While living in Batavia René, Bert, and I did not do as many things together. But I remember once the three of us went fishing at the ocean, the Bay of Batavia, with a throw net. René tried it and caught a big crab. He was excited and grabbed the crab not knowing how. One of the pinchers got him in a firm grip. René screamed bloody murder! The whole thing amused Bert and

me. We laughed so much I had trouble getting the claw loose to free René. We decided that was all the fishing for that day. But an Indonesian woman living close by felt sorry for René and invited us into her house for some rice with fish and fried egg and sweet soy sauce and a glass of iced tea. It was, in one word – delicious! We did not think we ever tasted such good food! René's pain was forgotten. We fished the rest of the afternoon.

**

The Indonesian people were always friendly to us. We could always climb a coconut tree and take some young coconuts, drink the water, and eat the sweet soft meat. Wherever we went we were invited into the bamboo huts of the people just as in Serang.

**

I did quite a bit of fishing and hunting all by myself. After school I often hunted and I shot lots of birds. Not knowing a thing yet of conservation I enjoyed it. There was a beautiful songbird, the size of a quail, black with yellow streaks and a yellow beak. The pregnant native women believed that if they ate that kind of bird they would get beautiful babies, so they begged me to shoot one for them, which I did. Lots of Indonesians were superstitious and believed in mythical figures.

**

We had school six days a week and Sunday was a day off, which I reserved for fishing. Initially I fished from the rocks at the ocean and later from a boat. Often I was invited by a friend of my father to go fishing at night at the ocean. We went by car to Tandjung Priok and fished from the rocks until about 10:00 P.M. It was fun.

Sometimes I went fishing with an Indonesian in his little row boat. At that time I had an allowance of ƒ2.50 (approx. $1.50). Everything was very cheap. I paid my Indonesian fishing partner in this way: I bought him breakfast, then dinner after fishing. That cost me about five cents. The meals included rice, fish, meat, a soup, vegetable, and coffee. Then I gave him a pack of cigarettes (10 sticks) and a quarter. He was as happy as a lark.

First we had to buy bait and did that at a fish shop. Live bait cost two cents. My partner knew the spots where the fish congregated. We caught all kinds of fish such as talking fish, bass, little sharks, blue crabs (very good to eat), and more. When we started to catch sharks, he lifted his anchor and moved to another spot, because, according to him, that meant the bigger sharks were around. Well, he was the boss.

The bottom of the ocean could be sandy, muddy, or rocky. When we were at a mud bottom we caught many sea snakes that were very poisonous. One time I thought I had a big fish on the line and I hauled it in. Close to the surface we saw something. I did not know what it was, but my partner knew. He pushed me aside and cut my fishing line. It was a big shark. Needless to say we left that spot. We often saw whales and large sharks, but we were never harmed. Many times I came home with well over a hundred fish that were seven to eight inches long. Made good meals!

**

There are a few islands in the bay, some of them good ones with beacons on them and people living there. Some friends and I would go there for fishing and swimming. One time while swimming I saw a huge shark swim by under me. I hauled myself onto the boat and told the other guys to get out of the water. It turned out to be a harmless basking shark, but I did not get in the water again. (Several years later, after I met Rika, she told me that she spent vacations, a week or two, with her sisters on one of the islands. They had a ball.)

**

EF: After we had lived on Struiswykstraat for about a year we moved a block away to an area called Salemba. Our house was across the street from the medical university and was formerly a place where the Masons got together. My pap was kind of a big shot in the Masons, though he never talked about what it was all about.

73

The natives called our house "Rumah Setan" - the house of the devil. They were afraid of it because they thought it was haunted. We encountered many unusual phenomena in that house.

The archipelago of Indonesia was rife with superstitions, woven into the fabric of the native culture for eons. The Indo-Europeans, however, were less prone to base their lives and actions on such fears, but one can easily imagine, with all the beliefs imbedded in the local customs, that, as with all societies, a few common irrationalities were often spoken of or adhered to rather to be safe than sorry.

There is no evidence that superstitions played a major role in the life of any individual Flissinger or Luikens, but one story has been handed down regarding the house in Salemba: During a particular period of time a number of the inhabitants - family members and servants – were all too frequently suffering from illnesses. A local shaman or witchdoctor was brought to the property. He performed his ritual in and around the house, and his "exorcism", it appeared, resolved the problem of the illnesses.

**

I have fond memories of the time we spent in the Salemba house. European people had servants to do the daily chores. When the servants were with a family for a while they became part of the family. They even idolized the children and took very good care of them. It was

74

such a nice period. Peaceful. People were very content.

The house was quite large - ten rooms – and each of us six boys had his own bedroom. There was a big kitchen where our "Kokki" (cook) did the daily meals. The bathroom had a huge cement tub in it, about 1000 liters, filled daily with well water by our djongos, a servant who took care of the yard and other "manly" jobs. The toilets were in a separate room. There were three faucets with running water in the house. For my mam's foodstuff and other goodies there was a big storage room. This gudang was always locked and Mam had the keys.

At the front of the house was one veranda and on the side of the house another. There was a deep well outside surrounded by a six-foot wall. The water was brought into the house for consumption and bathing and for a female servant to do the laundry. Almost all the houses in Indie had water wells. The villages had communal wells used by the natives.

There was also a pavilion - another house - on the property. We did not use it so Pap rented it out to a married couple. The husband was a veterinarian studying to become a doctor.

Our big yard had a variety of fruit trees - avocado, mango, banana, coconut, and guava, to name a few. We also had ducks and chickens. There were neighbors' cats, too, and we hated them because they were always trying to get at birds we had.

We had a happy and sheltered life. For René,

Bert, and me sports occupied a good deal of our time. Bert was an athlete and René a bicycle enthusiast. I pursued my swimming and high diving and became a member of the Mangaray Swim Team. We all did very well at our sports. We also did weight lifting and had weights up to 300 kg.

My days were filled with school, study at home, and sport activities. I even practiced swimming and high dive at night. School was from 7:00 a.m. until two in the afternoon. Then we had lunch, followed by a rest period that I did not take. Instead I did sports. I hit the books at 4:00 p.m. until dinner time at 8:00 p.m. After dinner I did more sports, and then my studies took me sometimes to three or four o'clock in the morning.

Dinner at our house was 8:00 p.m. <u>sharp</u>. A few minutes late meant no dinner and to bed with an empty stomach. This didn't happen too often, but when it did our "inside" male servant clandestinely brought us dinner.

Because we boys had our own rooms we took care of them our own way. Willie's room was the biggest. He had a double bed and he decided that some of the space in his bed could be utilized. He liked motorcycles. He put a motorcycle engine in his bed and still had enough room to sleep in it.

In 1934 I started my sport boxing. I needed a punching bag and room to practice. Since Willie's room was the biggest, we decided my punching bag should be in there. Soon we had all kinds of friends who wanted to learn and practice.

I got pocket money from Pap - ƒ2.50 a week. I paid seventy-five cents for my boxing lessons, fifty cents for swimming, and the rest for snacks. I had free gym lessons at school in the afternoons after classes.

As I got older, about seventeen, I kind of pulled away from the many sports I participated in, except boxing and swimming. (Swimming I did on a daily basis until 1939. Boxing I did for quite a while longer and later I resorted to practicing just the exercises, up until the mid-1980s.)

* * * * * *

On September 12, 1934, Rika's brother, Wolter Luikens married his long-time girlfriend, Marie van der Torren, likely in the city of Padang, Sumatra, Marie's hometown.

18.

FOCUS

Late teenage years can afford choices and inspire decisions that motivate young adults and concentrate their endeavors. Rika and Nes were typical in this regard.

FF: In 1934, after my high school studies were over, I continued on at the Ursulinen Klooster for two more years in the teachers school.

✶✶✶✶✶✶

My teens were fairly normal. I had not been sick since I was twelve years old. René, Bert, and I were still together sometimes but we drifted somewhat apart due to different interests that we pursued. René went to ambacht (craft/trade) school and he became a bicycle racer. Bert went to mulo (middle/high) school and excelled in athletics.

In 1936 I was chosen to represent Indie in the Olympics in high dive. The day before we were to leave I was on my way to practice in Bandung. I was on a bike down a steep hill. The brakes did not work. The wall around the swimming pool stopped me, and in doing so, the left side of my face, head, and body were badly hurt. I did not get to go to the Olympics, which I regretted terribly, but I still went on swimming several more years.

Then there were the boxing matches. The best fight I had was in early 1936 for the Championship of the East in lightweight. My opponent was a very undisciplined fighter from Singapore. All he did was run away from me or offer me his back. I won, but it was not the way I wanted to.

I never used my skills in martial arts or boxing to beat up on people. In fact I was continually harassed and dared to fight. I never did, except for one time. An Indonesian boy in my class at school dared me to fight him. I asked him what for? He said just to fight and prove himself. This went on for about six months on a daily basis. He called me yellow, a coward, etc. Well, I gave in and we set a date after school. We had a whole bunch of onlookers from different schools. We chose as the "arena" a dead end street. Well, he kind of pranced around me to look for an opening to hit me. I saw an opening myself and hit him just once between the eyes and knocked him out for over half an hour. After that he did not dare to face me. When he saw me coming he sure made an effort to evade me.

I fought in many sports events in the ring and I had lots and lots of friends - at least that is what they said - proclaiming that they knew me. Most of them I never met. (I encountered a guy in America who asked me if I was the boxer. When I confirmed it, he said, "You were my idol and I went to all your matches." I had never met him in Indonesia.)

Due to my pursuit of a police career and also because of the corruption in the sport circle, I gave up fighting.

19.

SOME ENCHANTED EVENING

April 27, 1936. The stars must have aligned.

At the Flissinger home a party was on tap for René's seventeenth birthday. As Willie, René, and Bert were still friends with the Luikenses over on Struiswykstraat, they invited that family's youngest, Frederika, to join in the fun and games. Ernest was, of course, also in attendance. Despite their living side by side three years earlier, this was Nes and Rika's first encounter.

> *EF: Willie, René, and Bert had girlfriends. I was still by myself, not looking for a girlfriend. But there is where I met my Rika. It was love at first sight, I would say, and we have been together ever since.*
>
> *MFG: How old were you?*
>
> *EF: I was eighteen. Your mam was nineteen when I met her.*
>
> *MFG: Mom, was it love at first sight?*
>
> *EF: (laughingly) It was seventy years ago.*
>
> *MFG: Seriously, did you like him when you met him?*
>
> *FF: Yes.*

EF: From then on we met regularly. There were other suitors, but I was there to "fight" them off. It took about six months to get in love with each other, then I asked her to be my steady girlfriend and her answer was yes. From then on we were together.

**

Rika and I were very much in love and I was a jealous guy. I did not tolerate any other guy even looking at her.

Living next door to the Luikenses, in #13, the same house the Flissingers had occupied in 1933, was the Calicher family. One of the sons was the same age as Nes.

EF: There was this neighbor, Willie Calicher, who

came over to see Riek and her family. Well, I let him know that I was not too pleased with his being there. But the poor guy came back time and again. Ironically, we became good friends later in the military.

20.

LIGHT ON THEIR FEET

Nes and Rika had much in common: good family values and upbringing, good educations, and a love of athletics. Not a bad way for a budding romance to start.

Riek and I had lots of fun. She excelled in mathematics and was studying at that time to become a teacher. We studied together, which was an excuse just to be with each other. I was still active with my sports, but because Riek and I were spending more and more time together, the sports suffered, except for boxing because I had the gym at home and I always practiced and exercised that sport. Riek, too, was good in sports. We went together to many sporting events. She was very conditioned in korfball and she was particularly fast on her feet, so track had been her strong point in high school. People always admired her when she was running. She was so fast it looked like she was "floating" on the track.

I excelled in all sports. The problem was that I had to pay for them myself and all I got was my weekly allowance from Pap. My favorite sport was swimming so I gave that priority. I told my boxing coach that I could not pay the ƒ1.50 for boxing anymore and he said that he was going to coach me for free. But this did not last long. The coach had other boxers, some from wealthy parents. I was supposed to box them, but my instructions were to just defend myself and never to hit back. I was more or less used as a punching bag. There was this big, strong, rich guy who hit me everywhere he wanted as hard as he could just to vent his anger. Well, one day I lashed out and knocked him out. My coach got angry at me and I told him I had enough and I quit! My coach later apologized and asked me to come back, but I refused. I still boxed and instructed friends who came to our house to practice.

I tapered off my sports activities - high dive, boxing, judo - but I gave lessons in all that and I tutored anything that had figures in it, like algebra. You name it, I did it. And I was looking forward to wearing a uniform. What military branch it would be I did not know at that time.

21.

BROKEN HEARTS

It is not unusual for the youngest child to get a lot of attention and become especially endearing to other family members. Seven-year-old Tinus fit that mold.

Ever since my pap's retirement he had been devoting most of his time to my youngest brother. Tinus was a skinny, blond boy who was my pap's favorite. Every afternoon he took a nap with Pap, and there he would write on the bed sheet the alphabet and his early math, to the delight of Pap.

Tinus had also grown to become a joy to me. When I came home he always greeted me at the front of the house with open arms and a kiss. Then I would pick him up and carry him into the house. When I was home, Tinus was always with me. He was my help and inspiration. Why, I do not know, but there was a mutual bond between us.

We had two large German shepherds in our house. They were very timid, shy, even afraid. One day the mailman came. Tinus ran to meet him and fell. Immediately the dogs attacked. The male dog pinned the mailman to the ground and had him by the throat. The skin was not broken but the dog growled. The female just stood there and looked on. The mailman was able to free himself, but, needless to say, he was very careful from then on.

One evening in 1936 I came home from sports. Pap was reading a paper on the front veranda and Tinus was lying on the ground. He did not come up to me as usual and I picked him up and kissed him. He felt very warm to the touch and appeared to have a high fever. I told Pap and an ambulance was called. Within minutes Tinus was taken to the hospital. The diagnosis: double pneumonia. Doctors struggled to treat him. Finally one doctor decided to tap his lungs, but Tinus, at seven years old, said, "No more, doctor. It is too late." After several days in the hospital Tinus died [August 20].

I could not comprehend and I cannot describe the sense of loss which anybody must feel at such a moment. Boy, did I miss him after he passed.

MFG: If he'd had it today they could have saved him, but back then?

EF: No, they didn't have the medications back then.

For Pap it was a severe blow because Tinus was his youngest and Pap had been with him so much during the past several years. We were afraid Pap was going crazy. He walked through the house mumbling, "Why, why? Why did this happen to me?" and did nothing but cry. He locked himself up and would not talk to anybody for about six months. He finally got out of the depression, but he was looking for the reason why Tinus was taken away from him. He became religious and, to our amazement, developed "powers", abilities to cure people with occult science. He became a member of the Rosecrucian. People would come to him for healing. He would help them only if they had a letter from their doctor stating they could not be cured. I know of cases where he cured deaf people, people with eye trouble, etc. He became well known in later years as a man with psychic powers.

✳✳✳✳

Klaas (Opa) Decker also died in 1936. I had only known him a short while. It was a blow to the Luikens family when this friend passed on.

22.

IN A CLASS OF HER OWN

Upon completion of her education in The Netherlands, Sister Alexia returned to Java and the Sisters Ursulinen. In addition to her original vows of service to God and the Catholic Church, Sister Alexia now devoted her life to teaching in the Catholic schools in and around Batavia.

Meanwhile, Frederika, still bent on a career as a teacher, encountered a slight detour in the process.

FF: In 1936 I left Ursulinen teachers school because I didn't pass a grade. The nun was talking to me and she said, "The inspector tells me (this and that). What do you think I should do?"

I said, "You should do what the inspector told you." I guess that was not the right thing to say.

I figured they didn't want me anymore at Ursulinen, so, to finish my studies to become a teacher, I went for one year to Carpenter Alting [a man the school was named after] Stichting [organization] Teachers College.

MG: How did your teaching schools differ from your high school?

FF: Well, you get ready to be a teacher. You have your languages that they teach you. And of course the regular other studies.

MG: You didn't know at that time whether you'd be teaching in private or public or government schools, did you?

FF: No. When you are ready, it depends on who hires you. It could be the government or private industry.

Frederika completed teachers college in 1937 and became a school teacher for grades one through seven. The typical school year was from August to May, with June and July being vacation time.

EF: She landed her first job at a non-government elementary school in a little town called Tegal.

FF: In middle Java.

MG: Were you teaching natives?

FF: Mostly Chinese.

MG: And what language did they speak?

FF: Dutch. Because I didn't speak any other language. I worked there for one year.

MG: Where did you live?

FF: I boarded with a family I knew who used to live on Struiswykstraat in Batavia.

After her first year of teaching in Tegal, Rika landed a job at a government school and came back to Batavia to teach. She was very stern but had high marks as a teacher and she was loved by her students and co-workers.

MG: When you were away for a year, did you know it was only going to be for one year?

FF: I don't know, I was not thinking that far. The schooling is about ten months, then you got a big vacation. When it came time for the vacation I found I could get a job closer to home. So I came back to Batavia and worked there at the government schools.

MG: You taught everything in Dutch. Were all the students in the government school actually Dutch children from Dutch families?

FF: There were Indonesian children also. And Chinese.

✳✳✳✳

After finishing college, Rika's brother, Wolter, had gone to work for a shipping company. A transfer took him and wife, Marie, to the small island of Banda Neira. They had their first child, Johannes (Han) Luikens, there on April 30, 1937.

23.

ON THE STREETS

The three musketeers were growing stronger and more accomplished and versatile. They began really stretching their muscles.

In Batavia we rode bikes. Pap had a car but we were not allowed to drive it yet. We used the bikes to go anyplace. We even pedaled to Sukabumi, Buitersorg, and Bandung, about four hundred miles away. There were steep hills in the mountains, but we managed.

René developed into quite a bicycle racer. On Struiswykstraat there was a bridge over a small stream. The bridge had real narrow, two-inch railings. Well, René put the tires of the bike on one of the railings, sat on the bike, and pedaled over the stream. We all were afraid he would fall off, but he made it.

René had a very rich, "millionaire" Chinese friend who bought him all kinds of things, once even a beautiful, light-weight bicycle. But this friend, nicknamed Karel Telir because his eyes were crossed, had something mentally wrong with him. He liked to gamble. It didn't take long and he lost all his money. The roles were then reversed. René became the "richer" of the two.

René, Bert and I were quite good in jujitsu. We heard that on a certain street a white woman was attacked by some Indonesians. René could not resist the challenge. He got an old dress of my mam, some pillows, a wig, lipstick, and rouge, dressed himself, put makeup on, put on the wig, and walked to the spot where he could expect to be attacked. It was after 7:00 p.m. and quite dark. Bert and I followed at a distance. After a short while we heard swearing in Dutch, screaming in Indonesian, and running footsteps. He hit three guys pretty hard. Those guys did not know what hit them. It never happened again.

I could go on telling stories about René and his antics. Not a day went by without something happening.

We participated in some organized marches, just for the sport and not for a certain purpose. We had no sponsors. The distances walked were twenty, twenty-five, and fifty miles. We did that once a week till we had walked all the phases. Finished them all.

René, Bert, and I were not doing mischief so much anymore. We had our friends and were interested in different sports. But we came together when I was instructing young guys in boxing and jujitsu. Willie's bedroom, with the hanging punching bag, was our gym. For actual practice we used our large living room. There the guys had a lot of fun beating up on each other. The boxing gloves we used were ten and twelve ounces. Kind of heavy after a while.

Bert had a best friend, Nieco Wedemeyer. He was 6'6" tall and weighed well over two hundred pounds. He wanted to master the sport of boxing. He liked it so much that he wanted to perform in the ring. We were training very hard and he could punch, so a match was set up. But in the ring Nieco had stage fright and he got beaten by a less qualified opponent. After that Nieco just came to practice. He rode his bike to our house with his gloves over the handle bars. One time he was mocked by Indonesians and they started to pick a fight with him. It didn't take long for Nieco to knock four guys to the ground. As a result there was an article in the paper and a headline the rough translation of which was "You fool around with me and I will fool around with you."

**

I had a good friend and swimming buddy named Boy Foret. We visited each other at each other's home. One day we were pedaling on our bikes to the swimming pool. Boy was not complaining about being sick but two days later he died of the zwarte koorts (black fever). I was never one who would attach himself to a person and call him my buddy (except my younger brothers at particular times). I had lots of fair weather friends. But the passing on of this friend affected me.

**

Nes was certainly growing into an outstanding young

man. His principles and sensibilities were maturing. This was manifested in, among many other ways, a close attachment to Marie's youngest son, Wolter van der Torren. Without a father figure in his life, Wolter was pleased to have Nes's attention and support. Whenever he could, Nes included the boy in fishing and other outdoor activities. Their bond grew strong.

**

As Nes and Rika became more and more entwined as a couple, Nes was moved to follow a growing urge. He had grown up in a family that had practiced no particular religion. But, as Rika was a devout Catholic, he began accompanying her to weekly masses. Knowing that he intended to spend the rest of his life with Rika, Nes made the decision to be baptized and joined her in the Catholic faith.

24.

A GOOD FISH STORY

Not everyone understands the allure of casting a line or net into the water, but Nes spent many a pleasurable hour in pursuit of the ever elusive fish.

I was still enjoying fishing. One time while Rika was away teaching in Tegal, I borrowed a sloop with sails and oars. It was an open boat. I got four other strong friends together and we were going to sail to the Thousand Islands outside the Bay of Batavia. When we got ready at the harbor, a Coast Guard officer came to us and asked us where we were going. We told him to the Thousand Islands. It was late afternoon. He said, "I would not do it. A big storm is coming up." But we knew better. After all, we were five strong athletes with a big boat (and no brains!). What could happen to us?

About one hour out in the bay the storm came up. We had a very good speed and we loved it. But the speed of the boat increased and the waves got bigger and bigger and finally they were huge. We stumbled to get the main sail down and used only the small sail. It was dark and all of a sudden we heard a big crash and we were in the water. We landed on a coral reef and, luckily, close to an island. We were bleeding profusely because our shins were cut open by the sharp coral. We made it to the beach as soon as we could and sat the night out on the beach.

By daylight we could see what had happened. There were only slats of the sloop left. Together we tried as much as we could to put it on the beach. We lost our utensils and fishing gear, everything. After a while we walked around the island to see if there was a shelter and some food to be found. Fortunately there was a beacon on the island and to our surprise there was a caretaker. He had food and water only for himself and not for hungry "sailors". He allowed us to sleep in the tower. There was no radio, no communication whatsoever with Batavia or any place else. For us it was: wait until they miss us at home.

We found a tree that was loaded with sweet fruit, purple in color and with large seeds. We could only eat the fruit around the seed (thin layer) but it did not take long for the five of us to eat the fruit. Understandably, all that we excreted was purple and we went like birds. It was funny, I guess, because we were confident that somebody would find us.

We noticed that we lost lots of strength and weight. On the fourth day after the accident a sloop landed on the island and an angry marine officer came up to us and almost screamed, "What are you guys doing on this island? It's restricted!" We showed him and told him what had happened. He ordered, "Get on the (marine) sloop and we will take you back on the marine patrol boat."

We had a good meal on board ship. It so happened that our parents were scared that something had happened and had a plane search party organized. The Coast Guard employee had remembered five guys going out in an open boat in a storm with intentions to go many miles away to the Thousand Islands, so the Coast Guard was alerted and we were found. At home there was scolding and actually nothing worse. Naturally our parents were glad to see us.

25.

A MAN IN UNIFORM

Ernest never confided what inspired him to be a policeman. Perhaps the knowledge that it was a very hazardous vocation caused him to spare his loved ones the details.

> *FF: I remember that a lot of young men wanted to be policemen. They could get good career training, and also being a policeman paid well.*

In 1937 I applied to the Police Academy in Sukabumi for the study of police inspector. The course would take two years. I decided I was going to be a commissioner of police before the age of thirty. To my disappointment I was not accepted. I could come back in six months for another try, which I did. My application was denied a second time. Why I was not accepted I did not know.

**

Every male at eighteen years of age had to register with the army. There was a draft instituted. In 1937 the military called me to perform my mandatory duties as a milicien [conscript]. (Some men tried to dodge the draft. They were mainly sons of rich parents. These dodgers went to Holland or other European countries to further their studies and during WWII with Germany they were in the middle of it and many were drafted anyway.)

After a few months I was offered the opportunity to go to officer training. I turned it down because, one, I wanted to be a police officer and, two, I did not really like the military. Even so, I did my best in the army with good results.

It turned out that Willie Calicher, my "rival" for Rika's hand, was drafted at the same time. Surprisingly we got to know each other better and became good friends during the year and a half we served together. In fact, there was not a thing he wouldn't do for me. You might say he took care of me.

We both became sergeants and enjoyed trying to outdo each other when we were out on patrols with our platoons. We were constantly picking on each other for the smallest things when one of us was in command. But whenever we went on exercises in the jungle for two weeks, he did all possible to please me. We were always together and had a tremendously good time. In the evenings Willie and I would sit on the bank of the river that ran through our camp and watch the monitor lizards running around and jumping from the trees into the river.

**

Once while on exercise in the jungle I shot a

python. I skinned the snake and found two claws close to the anal opening of the skin. These were rudimentary legs and were useful in hanging from trees. If the snake sensed animal heat and the prey was under it, it dropped itself on the prey and strangled it.

In camp were Indonesians of many different races. These people had lots of superstitions about lots of things. One was the belief that the possession of these python claws gave a man strength, virility, and power, in particular over women. A few days after I found the claws I was approached by an Ambonese soldier and he asked me if I was willing to sell them to him. I refused because it was a rarity. One day I went to take a shower and left my wallet under my pillow. I had the claws in my wallet. I also had lots of money in the wallet. When I came back from the shower I found that the claws were missing. All the money was intact. I knew who had taken the claws but could not prove it.

**

There were lots of wild pigs, deer, and other kinds of animals that we hunted. One day a Dutch soldier was hunting on a footpath to the barracks. He encountered a wild boar, shot it, but only wounded it. The boar attacked him. The man got scared and, instead of taking a second shot, he turned and ran. Then he fell. Soon the boar was on him. Before the animal was killed by another soldier it ripped the fallen soldier's face open with its tusks. Fortunately the soldier survived.

**

On night watch it got really quiet. Except for the mosquitos and the sound of other bugs flying around there was no sound. Some soldiers and I played cards and drank strong coffee to stay awake. At 6 a.m. we were relieved and by 8 a.m. we had to go on patrol or on military exercises. I sure enjoyed these things and they stuck with me.

26.

FORTITUDE: THE RIGHT STUFF

Rejection in no way diminished Nes's determination to pursue police work as a career.

> While I was in the army I made a third attempt to be accepted at the Police Academy. Again I was denied. But I would not give up. And then a fourth time my application was denied. My father, being a master in the Masons and knowing lots of influential people, wanted to help me and talk to the police chiefs. But I told him that I wanted to make it on my own. So I started checking out why I was rejected. It was not my written exam, but I stumbled always on the verbal test. At that time I must have shown some insecurity.

****

On September 23, 1938, in Surabaya, Rosalie Cramer Flissinger, Oma Rose, passed away at the age of seventy. (It was likely she was a widow at the time, but no family records note the passing of Opa Pede, Frederich Wilhelm Flissinger.)

****

Willie Calicher and I got out of the service in 1939. Willie was determined to become an airplane pilot. My sights were still set on being a policeman. I applied to Police Academy - for the fifth time. I was rejected once again. But one of the examiners said to me, "You are persistent. Are you going to be back next time?" My answer was affirmative.

Six months later I applied a sixth time and received rejection number six. But this time I found out why. They said it was because I had been a boxer and had had contests. I felt it was a lame reason.

****

In 1939 Frans and Martina, perhaps hoping to ameliorate the terrible loss of their youngest son, Tinus, anxiously awaited the birth of their ninth child. To their great dismay a baby girl was stillborn.

****

By 1940 Ernest had been applying to the Police Academy every six months for three years.

> *EF: On the seventh try I came face to face with the same examiner. This time he said, "You are very persistent by coming back year after year". Then he told me that it was unbecoming for a police officer to be a boxer competing at sporting events. I told him that I was not a professional,*

and besides, it would be beneficial for a police officer to be good at sports and be in perfect shape physically. Finally the examiner asked me, "If we flunk you this time, are you going to come back next year?" I said, "Yes. I want this job and I'm pretty good."

I got the job! I would start my training in July, 1940 to become an Inspector of Police!

MFG: And Mom was still teaching?

EF: Yes, she was teaching with the government

in Batavia.

MFG: Then you left.

EF: It was only a couple hours away, in Sukabumi, in West Java.

Sukabumi is in the mountains, about fifty miles south of Batavia. There were cars but I went by train. While I was in Sukabumi I boarded with an older couple that already boarded some of the other aspirant inspectors. I made new friends. It was fun. Breakfasts and dinners were served at the house and it always was a noisy affair. Every morning we had to commute to our classes. The academy was on the top of a rather steep hill so it was a bit of a climb to get there.

****

Wolter Luikens had been transferred by his employer back from Banda Neira to Batavia when he and Marie gave birth to their second son, Wolter Luikens, born July 8, 1940.

27.

THE INVASION

On December 7, 1941, Japanese war planes attacked the United States Naval Base at Pearl Harbor in Hawaii. Much of the world - including Indonesia - would never be the same.

EF: Early in the morning on December 8, I and my colleagues were at the boarding house. The radio was on and suddenly we heard the Dutch national anthem, "Wilhelmus". We all stood at attention. We knew something was going to be announced. Our Dutch Queen, Wilhelmina, spoke. The Netherlands was already at war with Germany, and since Japan had allied itself with Germany and bombed Pearl Harbor, The Netherlands, an ally of America, was declaring war on Japan as well. It was a solemn moment.

MFG: Did you hear that, too, Mom?

FF: Yes.

MG: How far along in the police academy were you when the war started?

EF: A year and a half. I had already the rank of inspector.

MG: It was after that that the Japanese came

your way?

EF: *We were confident that the Japs could never reach the islands where we were and that they would surrender in about three months. We thought we were strong, unbeatable. Were we ever mistaken.*

A few days later all the students at the academy were sent home. We were to report back in two weeks. But Rika and I had no idea what was going to happen, so on December 13, 1941, in Batavia, we got engaged.

****

Perhaps also feeling a sense of urgency Willie
Flissinger, in his naval uniform, married his fiancée, Rose
Kusiugan, in Batavia on December 29, 1941.

Willie (left) on his wedding day with brothers,
Bert, René, Ko, and Nes.

****

In early 1942 the Japanese invaded Indonesia.

> When the Japanese came, Willie, René, Bert, and I got caught up in it. Willie was an engineer on a Navy ship. His ship was torpedoed in the Bay of Bantam. We heard that he was captured, but we lost track of him for a good while.
>
> Bert was a sea observer in the Navy Air Service. He soon [March, 1942] got caught by the Japs and was transported to Japan where he was imprisoned at various labor camps for the duration of the war.

> *EF: René evacuated to Australia. He was then sent to Texas to train with the U.S. Air Force.*

> [From René's autobiographical writings:]
> "In 1941 I joined the N.E.I. [Netherlands East Indies] Air Force as cadet-pilot. In 1942, because of the war with Japan, I escaped to Australia with my squadron. I stayed there for seven weeks, then went with my squadron to America to training school where I received the rank of sergeant air gunner. I returned to Australia and in 1943 was stationed with the 18th Squadron, N.E.I. Air Force in Darwin [Northern Territory]."

Rika's brother, Wolter, was also moved to fight for his country. He joined the Dutch Navy. Unfortunately it wasn't long before he was captured and taken to a Japanese prison in Singapore.

FF: When the war broke out, he left. I asked him why he was going. He said, "I have to."

We heard about Willie Calicher, too. He had indeed become a pilot and flew planes in private life. When the war broke out he joined the Air Force. On his first mission to defend his country his plane was shot down in the Strait of Malacca, between Sumatra and the Malay Peninsula. It was later confirmed that he lost his life. It was such a shame. He was only 25 years old. I have fond memories of him. When we were on patrol in the army we often sat on the bank of a river looking at and listening to the birds. This was the first war fatality of someone we knew. He was a good friend.

****

Willem van der Torren, the estranged husband of Rika's sister, Marie, was living in Sumatra when the war broke out. According to accounts that came Marie's way after the war, a group of Dutch men had established an underground resistance movement there in Sumatra. Unfortunately, one of the rebels, likely in fear of Japanese reprisal, disclosed the group to the invaders. The group was rounded up and taken to Singapore where all, including Willem, were executed.

28.

THE HORROR

Those who have not experienced war first-hand will never fully comprehend the gut-wrenching emotions that soldiers and civilian victims and witnesses suffer during and after the traumas of such conflict. Ernest, as a policeman, saw more than his share of atrocities.

EF: Early one morning all the police students were lined up at attention in front of the Academy before classes. We heard a droning sound and looked up and saw planes flying over. They were kind of high up. I saw little things dropping from the planes. A short time later we heard the loud sounds of bombs. Jap airplanes had dropped their cargo. Everybody scrambled to safety, but there was no need because the Jap planes didn't come back.

At that time I was boarding in another house, living with two old ladies and a friend of mine. The explosions came from the direction of that house. We students got our orders and were dispersed over the area. I went down to the boarding house. In the yard I found little hands and feet and other body parts of children who were blown to pieces by the bombs. Across the street from the house, about 300 yards away, was a primary school. It turned out that the school was bombed. It was utter chaos. Soon parents, family members, and friends were looking for their little children. What a waste of life. It was my first experience with mass murder and the true suffering of people who lost a loved one. I never expected to see something like children being murdered in cold blood. And in the chaos were other children who were not hurt but lost. They did not know what happened. They were disoriented and went somewhere where they would not hear and see the unspeakable. This was the first time I had witnessed bombing and the killing of people. It was gruesome and a shock.

MG: Do you know why they bombed that particular village?

EF: We don't know why they did it. It was very terrible that we were attacked, but we were confident that we were going to make it ourselves, the Dutch, I mean. It turned out differently. That first bombing was just a preview of what was going to happen. I never could have imagined that human beings could be as cruel and unfeeling as what was displayed in the following three and a half years, which was nothing but two words: absolute hell. Even after more than fifty years it plagues and bothers me.

29.

THE TAKEOVER

Batavia fell on March 5, 1942, and the Dutch formally surrendered on March 9. Batavia was renamed Jakarta, essentially returning it to its Indonesian heritage. The islands of the archipelago were soon overrun by Japanese military forces. Prisons and concentration camps were established to intern the Dutch and other foreign nationals and the invaders began rounding up many European and American men, women, and children over twelve years old. Those not interned were under debilitating restrictions. They were not allowed to purchase food, to work, to have schools, or to listen to radios, news, or other information from the outside world. And no gatherings of people in any numbers. The rule of the colony was now in the hands of the Japanese.

> *FF: Shortly after our government capitulated, the Japanese closed all the government schools. I was no longer allowed to teach. Struiswykstraat, our street, became kind of famous because the Japanese used that street - there was a jail on the back of that street.*

****

Because the Dutch were no longer allowed to work,

Frederika's sister, Sophia, came back home to live with her mother and the rest of the family on Struiswykstraat. She was unmarried and had been working in the private sector for a number of years as a research analyst in Surabaya.

****

At the police academy we got orders to turn in our weapons but to stay on the force and on duty where we were stationed in Sukabumi. We were just an authority figure to keep the peace. The reason was that the Indonesians were rising up against the Dutch. The Japanese, who wanted the native populace on their side, riled up the Indonesians against the Dutch who had been their colonial masters for over 300 years. The people changed overnight from good to sometimes demons. There were individuals, of course, who stayed loyal to the Dutch. Servants who were in families for a long time stayed with them. But the situation got very bad. Many Dutch, especially the women, were betrayed by Indonesians. Indonesian boys would go by our houses and point out to the Japs, "Here are Dutch women, there are Dutch women." Some of the women were forcibly taken and raped or murdered. The atrocities that the Japs and the Indonesians committed against us were just out of this world. And there were traitors among some European women who gave themselves to the Japs. It might have been so they could stay out of concentration camps or get extra favors or food, but some of them were just -----.

I had to stay on duty without weapons and we saw the cruelest things the Japanese did. Right away when the Jap military arrived in Sukabumi they set up a brothel in a two-story Victorian mansion just across from police headquarters. Our police had been under the direct command of a controller of the Dutch Department of the Interior. Because the Japs could not get enough Indonesian prostitutes and women to satisfy their needs, this controller was ordered by the Japanese to go to the intern camps and prison camps and ask for Dutch, American, and English women who would give themselves as prostitutes for the Japs. But instead of looking for women under the specified races, the controller found some German women and delivered them to the brothel. Soon it was found out, and just for this fact the man was shot pointblank in the head and his body was thrown in the street in front of his house. It was put there to show "the people" what would happen if the Japs were crossed.

The body was in the street in the baking sun, about 110 degrees. I drove by on my motorcycle and saw the situation. I decided to go home and get a bed sheet to cover up the man. When I returned I saw he had had stones and rocks thrown at him. When I tried to put the bed sheet over him, a Jap, pistol drawn, approached and threatened to kill me if I did what I intended to do. He called me "dog". There were lots of Indonesian onlookers cheering. The body remained there for four days until decomposition had advanced.

EF: We saw cruelty after cruelty. Slapping around the head was a regular punishment for not giving the Japs full respect when the people met a Jap. Killing was also the order of the day. And rape was the thing. I saw women, many months pregnant, being raped in the street in open sight of the public. One eight-month pregnant woman was raped at a bus stop. After the act the perpetrator plunged his bayonet into the victim's stomach, killing the mother and baby. It was a horrible thing.

But many Indonesians came to experience that the Japs were just as brutal to the Indonesians. It did not take them long to wake up and realize what they had on their hands with the Japs. They did not want the Dutch, but the Japs were worse. There were riots all over. We had to suppress the situations without weapons, just rubber night sticks. The rulers, however, were different. They just shot. Rumors were that the Indonesians in Bantam (West Java), in particular Lai Serang, were restless. What the Japs did was instigate a riot by insulting the people of the Moslem faith. The Japs slaughtered a pig (biggest insult ever) in a house of Moslem religion. There was an immense uprising, thousands of people in a big group together. The Japs fired machine guns and thousands were killed. After that no more riots. The rulers used examples like this to get the fear in the people and control them. The Japs' barbaric attitude and behavior sure changed the thinking of many Indonesians toward the Dutch, for the better.

**

There was in the hills of Sukabumi an intern camp for captured Dutch citizens. The imprisoned were of all ages. Some were from that area. A couple of young men got acquainted with and befriended a Jap soldier. This soldier allowed the boys to go out of camp every night after roll call with the understanding that they would be back at daybreak before the morning count of prisoners. All went well for about two weeks. One day the boys returned and there was a surprise. The guard had been changed. The boys had to stay outside. The new guard did not know or see a thing. But an Indonesian saw what was happening and reported the "escape". There was panic and the search was on. They were not to be found. Then the police were ordered to look for the boys and catch them. Some of my colleagues and I knew where they were hiding and did not do much to find them. But a higher ranking police officer searched them out and delivered them to the Japs. The boys were tortured in full view of all the persons in camp. The boys spat on the torturers. Finally they were beheaded. It was absolutely cruel and very sad.

(I reported this case and the police officer to the Dutch authorities after the war. There was an inquest but I was not called upon. I met the bastard once after the war. I was his superior then. He said to me, "Well, I got out of it. They could not prove a thing." If I had known about the inquest I sure would have done all that was possible to punish this -----! Water under the bridge.)

∗∗

One time I stood guard at a railroad station. I had a beautiful ring on my left ring finger and a watch on my arm. A Korean serving in the Japanese army approached me. On both his arms he had fifteen or more wrist watches. This alone put me on the offensive. He told me in broken Malay that he wanted my ring and watch. I pretended that I could not get the ring off. That was no problem for him. He proceeded to draw his Samurai sword. Having seen the many recent atrocities I reacted immediately. With my skill as a jujitsu expert I applied a grip that could break an arm or neck. The man flipped and fell on his head. I didn't know if I broke his neck or killed him. Fearing the consequences I ran away as fast as I could. I never saw him again. I could never feel any sympathy for these people. Hatred is a more appropriate word.

∗∗

Another time I was driving my motorcycle which had a left side bucket. It was on a hilly terrain. Suddenly I was pursued by some Japs in their jeep. I was trying to get away from them. I made a left turn in the road and made the turn too fast. The bucket came up into the air and I lost control. The motorcycle hung up in the trees and I landed at the bottom of a ravine alongside a river. Later I learned that some Japs came down to the river to investigate. I was told that they kicked me to see if I was alive. They decided that I was a goner and left. Some natives later picked me up and took me to an Indonesian doctor. He put me on some planks in a straight position for two weeks. I had some damage to my spine and upper vertebrae. Finally I was released, apparently healed. But I suffered severe headaches and back pain for years after.

30.

WARTIME WEDDING

Even in the worst of times the heart and the head can stay on course for something positive, even exhilarating.

> *EF: Because the situation was so strained and we were not sure whether we would come out alive or would ever see each other again, Rika decided, "Let's get married. You never know what's happening to you, what's happening to me."*
>
> *FF: Also, I couldn't get married before, because the rule was that when you are a teacher for the government, you're not supposed to be married.*
>
> *MG: Why was that a rule?*
>
> *FF: I don't know, but that's why we didn't marry earlier. But then when the war broke out and I didn't have a job anymore, I said well, now we can get married.*
>
> *MFG: So you courted for how many years?*
>
> *EF: From 1936 - six years.*

Getting married was another matter forbidden by the Japanese.

> We could not get a permit and, anyway, we

did not have the money for the registration and permit, so we went to the Catholic priest in our diocese and explained our situation. The priest agreed to marry us.

On Wednesday, May 6, 1942, Ernest Flissinger and Frederika Luikens were married by Fr. H. Lunter in the local Catholic church, Sint Joseph Kerk (Pastorie Kramat) in Jakarta. (Because of the war restrictions, the couple was not able to register the marriage with the civil authorities until April 27, 1946.)

> The wedding was simple, in the presence of family and friends who were still free. Our witnesses were husband and wife, Wim and Sally Walburg. We only had bikes and a horse-drawn carriage for transportation.
>
> MG: Then you and Pop went back to Sukabumi where Pop was stationed?
>
> FF: Yes.
>
> MG: Where did you stay? Pop had been boarding there.
>
> FF: Yes, we lived with the other boarders there. But it was only for about a week.
>
> EF: Yes, all the European police officers were dismissed and told they could go home. We did not know what would befall us. I expected to be imprisoned when I got back to Jakarta.
> We left on the first train available. The ride

took several hours, arriving at the railroad station in Mangarai, a suburb of Jakarta. When I got off the train we were immediately confronted by a Jap military man. Before this man could ask a question, Riek said in Indonesian, "We are Indonesians."

The man looked at me suspiciously and said, "You Indonesian?"

I said, "Yes." He motioned for us to leave the station.

FF: They didn't know who was Dutch and who was Indonesian.

EF: So they let us go. It was very quick thinking of Riek.

****

During the initial weeks that René spent in Australia in 1942, his squadron was stationed at Parafield, a flight training airport just outside Adelaide in South Australia. One day a young lady, Rhonda Constance Feutrill, born in Port Wakefield, South Australia, on July 25, 1924, was walking with two girlfriends when a young, handsome airman (René) whistled at her. Romance was about to blossom!

31.

TOO CLOSE FOR COMFORT

After getting back from Sukabumi, the newlyweds went to live with Nes's parents. Also living with them were Willie's wife, Rose, and Ko's girlfriend, Leoni Mary van Buuren (born January 11, 1925). Leoni was pregnant at the time and, as it was inappropriate for two people to live together unless they were married, Ko was living with friends.

> FF: But after a week or so Mr. Flissinger, to combine everyone's limited resources, asked my mother if we could rent rooms in her house. My mother agreed and the Flissingers and Nes and I moved to Struiswykstraat No.11. Rose and Leoni went to live somewhere else [likely with family or friends].
>
> MG: Do you remember how Ko and Leoni met?
>
> FF: No.
>
> MG: Do you remember anything about Ko and Leoni getting married.
>
> FF: I think they got married in Singapore, but I'm not sure.
>
> MG: What makes you think Singapore?

FF: Well, Ko went to Singapore - I don't know if it was to get away or what - but I think they got married there. Then the baby was born - that was Jonnie.

Indeed, on September 9, 1942, Leoni gave birth to John Maarten Flissinger.

MG: Were there children from Willie and Rose?

FF: No, no children.

EF: In the house also were Riek's sisters, Jopie, Fietje, and Marie with her three children, Sonja, Roeland (Boetie), and Wolter.

FF: Because of the crowded conditions, Nes and I slept in the garage.

We started our married life during very depressing and dangerous times. The situation was tense and stressful. And living in close quarters, squabbles among the family were frequent. No money to buy things. No activities or socializing. No jobs. But we had to stay together and make the best of it.

32.

LIVING IN FEAR

It is hard to fathom the absolute reversal of fortune the Indo-Europeans had suffered. In just a few short months they had gone from elite to outcast. Their future was completely uncertain.

There was tremendous pressure from the Japanese and the Indonesians. We had to watch what we said, how we acted, who we talked to. We were continually on the look-out for danger and betrayal not only by the Indonesians but also by our own race and group. It was very dangerous to listen to the radio. There was hardly any communication with the outside world. There were rumors of U-boats landing on the islands in Indonesia. Some of the news trickled through to us. But the Japs got the smell of it and were very much on the alert. The war, which was supposed to last three months, had no end in sight.

Being human we did all the things that were "forbidden". I had a .22 caliber snub-nose gun hidden away. If detected the punishment would be very severe.

We were aware that the attitude of the Indonesians toward us Europeans had been changing in such a way that the Indonesians were not to be trusted. We had to be careful talking to each other when servants, or any Indonesians for that matter, were around. We heard that many "foreigners" were turned in to the Jap authorities for small infractions. The situation became tense and it took its toll on all of us. We lived in constant fear of being caught by the Japs.

EF: We stayed in our houses - we were allowed to do that, but nothing else. There were no jobs and therefore no income.

We were not allowed to purchase food because the Japs forbade the native people to sell food to the Dutch. Fortunately there were people who liked us and were loyal to us who smuggled us fruit and food hidden under rags and garbage. All we could do was barter, give our possessions, bit by bit, to live.

33.

INTERNMENT

Conquerors historically have used many methods to repress the conquered and human rights have hardly ever been an initial consideration. The Japanese were immediate in their approach to ruling and controlling their new subjects.

> *EF: Things didn't stay the same very long. In June the order came from the Japanese that all "foreigners", including women and children, had to report to the police departments in certain sections of Jakarta and register our nationalities with the Japs.*

> *FF: And a month or so later the Japanese came house to house to pick up the men who had registered.*

> *MG: Not the women?*

> *EF: Just the men.*

> *FF: In different cities women too. But in Batavia there were too many, so they let the women go.*

> *MG: And when you registered as Dutch, did you know they were going to arrest you?*

> *EF: Oh, yeah.*

In July my father and I were arrested. I was interned in the concentration camp called Bukit Duri in Mt. Cornelis, a town close to Jakarta. It was a regular prison. Pap was taken to a different camp, in Benu.

When I got into prison camp I was bewildered. Riek knew where I was, but we could not get in contact with each other. All contact with the outside world was nonexistent. I soon learned that the conditions in camp were deplorable. Cells built for two people held up to eight. My brother, Ko, was also in this prison. He had been picked up before me.

MFG: How many people were in the prison?

EF: There were already 2000 prisoners there varying in age from fifteen to eighty, but the majority were older people in their fifties and sixties.

FF: All men.

EF: Yes, all men. The older ones were all retired, and at that time fifty years, sixty years was very old.

MFG: What did they feed you?

EF: The food was just raw vegetables thrown together in hot water - and with bugs - butterflies, caterpillars, moths, flies. It was real bad. And the food situation got worse by the day. No meat or protein except the bugs. But it didn't make any difference, we had to eat it. That was all they gave us.

The food was brought out into the yard in fifty gallon drums. Right away I noticed that nobody was doing anything. I said, "There is food over there."

"We have to wait," I was told.

"Wait for what?" I asked.

"Well, there are some guys who will distribute the food."

Nobody moved. Then some young, tough prisoners came through the doors out into the yard. I asked, "What's going on here? Why don't we get the food?"

A tough guy said, "Oh, we distribute the food."

They helped themselves to the food first. After they ate what they wanted, the rest of the prisoners could help themselves. I learned that that group had terrorized the camp.

I was known there - I was a boxer - so I got together a group of six strong guys that I knew who also were trained in boxing and judo and we decided that the food situation should change. A few days later the food was brought out and we took positions. The tough guys came out and I told them that things had changed and that we would be taking over the distribution of the food.

"Who says?" they asked.

My group came forward and said, "We do."

"We are thrown together here not of our own will," I told the bullies, "and we have to make a go of it as best we can. Your reign is over and if you want to pursue it you will get the beating of your life." Believe it or not that was the end of it. From that time on the food was distributed equally.

I noticed other disturbing things. One was that there was no loyalty among the people towards each other. Sometimes sons even betrayed fathers, reporting them to the Japs. And often there were fights. One could attribute that to the stress and pressure, true, but I was surprised there was not more restraint.

The situation was "restless". I soon found out that people were sneaking out of prison at night to get some food. It was all hush-hush. Through the culverts in the draining system they left and came back. They had to be very careful that no native would betray them to the Japs. The result would have been disastrous. These people also had to watch out for the fellow prisoners who were very eager to report them to the prison guards to gain a favor for themselves. The slightest infraction and all two thousand in the camp were punished. Once, a man saw his wife in the street. He greeted her through the bars. This was found out and everybody had to take a blow to the head with a stick the size of a baseball bat.

The old people, mostly fifty years and older, were left to themselves and kind of neglected. I noticed they did not look too clean. They did not do laundry as they should. As there was lots of time to kill anyway, I decided to do their laundry for them. There was some selfishness in my reason. I certainly wanted to do what I could for those who couldn't help themselves, but also my hope was that I would be "repaid" by similar help and treatment somehow being given to my pap where he was imprisoned.

Concentration camp life was dangerous – and boring and monotonous. I saw and learned lots of things because we prisoners had so much time on our hands. But it was difficult to stay active. There was no reading material, no library. To keep busy we invented all kinds of physical and mental exercises.

Due to the terrible sanitary conditions and lack of medications, many diseases broke out. The worst was dysentery, a result of the bad food. It's a terrible, painful disease. All you do is go to the bathroom and all there is is blood, and there was no medication whatsoever. Everyone in the camp had it. It went like wildfire. Lots of people died, not only the older ones but also the younger. The only relief we had was drinking tea, as strong as we could have it. I was afflicted and feared the worst. Somehow I suffered through it.

34.

DESPERATE MEASURES

In January, 1943 Frederika made a daring move to rescue her husband.

MG: When did you think you had a way to get him out?

FF: Well, one of my backdoor neighbors told me that I could get a prisoner out if I did certain things, so I did what she told me. You had to prove whether he was Indonesian or German. Those were the two allies against us.

MG: So, if you were Indonesian or German, you could get out?

FF: And he was neither.

EF: Rika went to my mother who was still living in Mam Luikens's house and asked to see her Bible. In that Bible Rika found a prayer picture of my great-grandmother [likely Agatha Calvis Flissinger's mother]. She was German. Rika was so excited! She said, "I got it, I got it!" And so with that picture and a family tree that she made up showing the German descent, she went to the Japanese.

FF: I tried to get him out and I was very lucky.

MFG: Because you did what?

FF: I went a couple of times to the main headquarters of the Japanese soldiers. I had heard the name Kobayashi. I didn't know who he was or what he looked like.

EF: Or how important he was.

FF: They asked me who do you want to see? I said, "Kobayashi."
    They said, "Which one – the tall one or the short one?"
    I picked, "The tall one." And I just had the good luck to say the right thing.
    But they told me, "You cannot see him today, come back tomorrow."
    So the next day I came back again. A Japanese man wrote something on a piece of paper and gave it to me. I then went to the prison where Nes was and I showed the Japanese officers the piece of paper.

EF: She didn't know that the Japanese man who had written the note was such a big shot. He was the biggest boss that they had in that area.

MG: And they let you go?

EF: Some prison guards started calling out my name. My fellow prisoners told me, "Well, this is the end for you. You are a policeman and this is it. You are going to die."

We were realistic. We knew the possibility.

But even though we all expected that I would be killed, the guys said, "Will you do us a favor, if you get out? Notify our wives where we are."

I stood there four or five minutes as they put all kinds of notes to their wives in the hems of my pants and shirts, in my shoes even, for me to deliver if at all possible. I had forty-six of them on me. If the Japs had found out, the whole camp would have been in real bad trouble.

The prison guards got very anxious and nervous and kept calling my name. Finally I was ready and I was led in front of a big shot, a lieutenant. He said, "What you got in your clothes, dog?"

I got scared and probably was white as a sheet because I expected to be killed. I said, "I got my handkerchief and my rosary."

"Empty your pockets, dog." I did and had only the rosary and a hanky. "What is that?" the lieutenant asked, indicating the rosary.

I said, "That is the way I pray to my God. You pray to your God your way. I pray to mine my way."

Pointing to the huge prison doors about ten feet high, he said, "Get out, you dog!"

I didn't know what was happening. I expected to be shot in the back of the head for "attempted" escape. Instead a big Korean - must have been well over six feet tall - came up behind me, grabbed me by the seat of my pants, and threw me out the doors and onto the gravel outside the prison.

I couldn't see a thing, the sun was blinding. And it was about 110 degrees. Due to the dysentery I could barely walk. It took me about a half an hour to get adjusted. Then I saw somebody wave in the distance. It was Rika. She didn't dare come close. So, as soon as I could, I went to her.

MFG: How long were you in prison?

EF: About six months. Then Rika took me to a German doctor, Von Pays, her family doctor before the war. He treated me for two weeks with injections before the dysentery was conquered.

35.

FOOD ON THE TABLE

It certainly was a great relief to have Nes back home. But the challenges that lay ahead were still staggering.

> After Riek got me out of prison camp we still feared for our well-being. Not just for us but for Riek's whole family and my mother, too. It was always a question of staying out of prison.

MG: Were you underground?

FF: We lived openly because the women weren't picked up, not in Jakarta. In Bandung and other places they picked up women and men.

EF: And children.

MG: So, you could stay in your house if you were a woman, but Pop could have been picked up again?

EF: I was always afraid I was going to be picked up again.

> The Europeans who were allowed to stay out of concentration camps had to deal with all kinds of restrictions and constant pressures, such as getting food, safely, and keeping the women from being attacked by the Jap rulers. Incidentally, Orientals were under the same

pressure. I met a Chinese man and we became friends. We spoke English only. We stayed in contact for a while, but eventually we lost track of each other, as he lived in another part of town.

EF: We weren't allowed to make any money. Rika was not allowed to teach, I wasn't allowed to do anything. But we had to make a living, so we did it clandestinely.

FF: In our yard I taught lessons to children whose parents were spared the concentration camps.

MG: The other families paid you for teaching their children?

FF: The other families helped by giving things.

EF: And I managed to give lessons in boxing and jujitsu to youths, seventeen to twenty years old, all races, to protect themselves when sometimes it turned out to be necessary. And after a lesson I said, facetiously, "Now go out and beat up on the Japs. Approach them from all sides and beat the heck out of them." Sometimes they did.

MFG: It was a pretty violent life.

EF: Oh, yes. But actually there was no chance for us to do anything.

It was risky to have contact with others, and after some months our teaching activities became too dangerous. We had to do something else to make money so we started making condensed milk and sold it to people who were still "free". Very hard. Lots of spoilage, so we stopped.

And then at that time I met a cousin of mine, Ferry Cramer, a remote cousin. He was a medical student. He was going to be a doctor. And with him I went all over the country.

FF: They went by bicycle and they went out every day.

What we did, Cramer and I, was smuggle medical equipment and tools and medication. I collected medication and Cramer administered it, gave injections, to the people of Dutch descent in the underground.

MG: What did underground actually mean?

EF: Hidden in spots or in the villages. Anyplace they could.

FF: If they had come out in the open, they would have been picked up.

Cramer also administered medicine for free to the needy in the kampungs (villages). Medications came from the Australian underground and from Jap supplies. We stole from the Japs and sold back to them their own merchandise. We were very lucky we never got caught. Nobody was supposed to have any medications, not even aspirin. Everything had to be turned in to the Japs. If anyone was found in possession of even aspirin, one had to swallow a whole bottle, about twenty-five tablets, and die right there. Or another punishment might be to be put naked in a barbed wire cage, 4'x4'x6', in the hot sun with heat rising to 105-117 degrees, for all to see. A laughing stock for the Indonesian onlookers.

One time we had a message that Australian submarine men were going to come to a certain spot and I was going to get medication - quinine for malaria - from them. But before I went down there, I asked Rika for an old girdle. She asked why. I said, "Well, I don't feel good," which was a lie. I didn't want her to get excited or scared. I made pockets in the girdle. I was able to put more than fifty little capsules in there. If the Japs found me, they would have injected me with a whole capsule which would be an overdose and I would be killed on the spot.

The situation got worse day by day. Our only transportation was our bicycles. One day, after we had just received medications at Pasas Ikar, we got stopped at a roadblock. I had about sixty-five ampules of quinine on me. I had high boots on. Hidden in my right boot I had my police service gun. In my left boot was another gun. Cramer and I were ordered into the guard house. We said goodbye to each other, fearing the worst. I was pale like a sheet. So was Cramer.

We were brought before a Jap officer. But luck was with us. The Jap was a sympathetic guy. He said, "You look sick."

I said, "I don't feel good in my stomach."

To our great surprise he responded, "When you get home, have mother cook you fresh water clams in (such and such) way. Will cure you entirely. You go now."

I said, "Oh, thank you," and we left. They didn't search us because I complained of being sick! A half hour later we had to stop. We laughed so hard! We were grateful for our good luck and sure felt lots better then.

We kept on doing this for some time. But it was more and more apparent that there were two enemies - the Japs and the Indonesians. We could not even trust our servants.

36.

BEREAVEMENT

On July 27, 1943, a few days before her thirty-second birthday, Sophia (Fietje) Antonia Luikens passed away.

> *FF: Fietje had tuberculosis. TB was not so bad if there was medicine, but because of the war the medicine was not available.*

> *EF: How she got the TB - she was an analyst.*

> *FF: I cannot prove that she got the TB from working in research in Surabaya, but maybe. She didn't show signs of the disease until she was back in Jakarta. Anyway, she was sick for about a year and we lost her. She was a very smart woman.*

**

That same year Ernest got word about his brother, Willie, captured the year before during the Japanese invasion.

> *EF: One of his cabin boys told somebody who told us, "Your brother is on a convoy going from Buitensorg to Jakarta."*
>
> *MFG: Where is Buitensorg?*
>
> *EF: A little town out of Jakarta, in west Java. And a convoy came from there to Jakarta every day. We stood at the side of the road, Rika and I, and we saw him. And the only thing he could do was wink at us, because he did not dare wave. That would have been a death sentence for him and for us if the Japanese had seen it. So we are sure that we saw him, that it was him. But later we heard that he was beheaded by the Japanese. I don't know where. I think he was killed on an island – Seram - north of Ambon.* [Willie would have been twenty-seven that September.] *After the war Rika and I looked for his grave, but we couldn't find it.*

37.

UP TO HIS OLD TRICKS

In 1944 René, by then a squadron leader, was assigned to fly reconnaissance and bomber missions out of Australia.

> I have to tell a funny story of this guy, my younger brother, René. He asked for a month off to marry Ronda. He was told no. Now, René is a very smart guy. There was a tree outside the headquarters and René would talk to that tree and laugh. The commander thought René was going crazy. He sent a guy out there who asked René what was happening. René said, "You should hear the stories this tree is telling!" So René got his vacation for one month, because he pretended to be crazy!

On April 14, 1944, René Flissinger married Rhonda Feutrill in the Pirie Street Methodist Church in Adelaide, South Australia.

**

> [From René's autobiographical writings:]
> "At the end of 1944 I was stationed at Brisbane, Queensland, at the Dutch Headquarters where I was M.P. [military police]. Then I was transferred to the training school for pilots at Temora and at

Wagga Wagga, New South Wales. After several months training I received my pilots wing and rank of sergeant. I then joined the 19th Squadron in Bundaberg, flying the Mitchell bomber to the Pacific and back."

38.

THIS CLOSE

Fear was hardly the only emotion that permeated the demeanor of the suppressed. Anger was understandably pervasive.

One day in 1944 I was on my bicycle. I was stopped and ordered to go to a place run by the Japanese and Indonesians together. There some Indonesians, very much against the Dutch, said, "The Dutch, they now eat chicken food!"

I got mad and said, "We are not eating chicken food! We eat all kinds of food that we want! You eat chicken food!"

For that I got arrested. I got hit by one of my former sergeants and I got thrown in prison. The prison was designed by the Dutch for at most four people. There were fifteen in it. Some were dying, hardly moving, with bones sticking out of their chests, arms, and legs due to torture. I expected the same treatment and expected no food. There was no place for me to lie down. I sat in a corner – and I prayed. I prayed the rosary all day and night.

MFG: That was the rosary you got on that ship?

EF: Yes, from Pastor Molenaar. I sat there in the corner. It was so bleak. I was desperate. There was no chance to get out. I didn't know what to do. And Rika didn't know where I was.

Then, after several days, a guy rapped on the bars at night. And he said, "Sir, I got something for you." It was meat, fish, and rice.

I said, "Where did you get it?"

He said, "Eat it." If he had been found out, he would have been killed on the spot. He did it for four or five days.

MG: What nationality was he?

EF: He was Indonesian and Bouganese, from the island called Bouga which was very much Dutch oriented. Badaru was his name. After about five days, he said, "Can you give me your wife's address?" I thought why does he want my wife's address? Does he want to kill her? So I held off. But my hunger got worse and worse and I got weaker and weaker, so I finally told him. He went to Rika and said, "Your husband needs food, can you give me some money?" So Rika gave him some money and he brought me more food. He kept me alive that way for almost three weeks.

While I was imprisoned little boys, twelve, thirteen years old, came and had to take care of the urinal.

FF: They were imprisoned too.

EF: Yes, picked up by the Japs. They came up to me and said, "Sir, don't you worry. The war will be over soon." Those little guys finally died and went home in crates, just skin and bones.

147

Each day I was approached by a Jap with a blank piece of paper for me to sign. I didn't know what they wanted it for – a confession of some kind? This happened twice a day. I refused.

EF: One day Rika came to the prison and asked if she could see me. They said, "Why?"
"To let him know I am pregnant."
"How do you know you are pregnant?" was the nasty response.

FF: Actually Nes already knew I was pregnant, but I was hoping they would feel sympathy for us. But they didn't.

After several weeks I was called into the office of a captain. He was a former subordinate of mine. He spoke Dutch. He said, "Sir, can you sign this?"

"Sign what?" I asked.

It was a blank piece of paper. He said, "Put your signature on it."

I said, "What do you want with it?"

"We fill in later what we want with it."

I said, "No, I'm not going to sign that." He kept it up for two hours, walking in front of me. I said, "I'm not going to sign that. If you want to kill me, go ahead, but I'm not going to sign that."

To my surprise he finally said, "OK, I'm going to let you go."

I walked out of the prison. But I didn't trust his soldiers. I feared I would be shot in the back. So I walked toward the street - backwards - keeping the prison in sight. When I was close to the street I saw soldiers popping up with guns aimed at me. They couldn't shoot because I was then on a busy street. They would have hit others. When I was in the crowd I walked home. Rika, of course, asked me what happened. I said, "I don't know."

MG: So you don't know why you got out?

EF: No.

$**$

There was one more time that I was to be imprisoned. In late 1944 all Europeans, the men out of prison, had to report for lock-up. Cramer went with me. But luck was with us again. The Jap at the desk stupidly put our papers on the wrong stack - of people who were to be released! Cramer and I were let go! We went home and had a good laugh about it. Somebody was watching over us, that is for sure, through the whole war. But all in all there was nothing but suffering for the whole three and a half years.

39.

A SILVER LINING

Despite the terrible circumstances and hardship in Indonesia during this horrific war, there was at least one moment of joy. In Jakarta, on March 14, 1945, Ernest and Frederika greeted their firstborn child, Marguerite Jacqueline Flissinger. She was nicknamed Maja (pronounced my-uh), from the first two letters of her first and middle names.

> *MG: When you gave birth to Maja, where were the two of you?*

> *FF: Still on Struiswykstraat. But Maja was born in a hospital. We had a midwife.*

40.

THE BOMBS

On May 8, 1945, Germany surrendered to the Allied Forces in Europe, but the war in the Pacific raged on.

We continually needed money but of course there were no jobs. Then one day I learned that the Japs needed an auto mechanic. I applied. The Japs said, "OK, here's a truck, the thing doesn't run."

Fear grabbed me again. I didn't know a thing about trucks. I didn't know a thing about cars. But I jerked this wire and jerked that wire, and I said, "OK, start it." And the thing started! It ran like a top!

The Japs said, "OK, you're hired."

So I worked there at the auto shop for a short time before the end of the war. And while I was there I met an Indonesian. He was in a wheelchair and I felt sorry for him. I trusted him and took him with me to all kinds of spots. We made maps of the Japanese - where they had their ammunition - and I made a report on it to the underground. But that guy betrayed me - the little bastard. Sorry to use the word, but that is the truth. He went to the Japs.

The Japs said, "You're an American spy - admit it!"

I denied it all, "If you have proof, prove it."

They said, "So, we'll have to kill you." There were three officers around me ready to chop my head off.

But then one of them said, "No, we made a mistake, can we take you home in our car?"

I said, "In your car? Three and a half years I have cooperated with you and now you want to take me home in your car? No way, no thank you." So I walked home. Once again, I don't know how, I had avoided a terrible outcome.

**

On July 26, 1945, the United States along with Great Britain and China issued the Potsdam Declaration, outlining terms of surrender for Japan. The Japanese, however, would not give up.

On August 6, an American B-29 bomber dropped an atomic bomb on the city of Hiroshima, Japan. Emperor Hirohito, despite the unprecedented destruction and loss of lives at Hiroshima, still refused to surrender. Three days later, on August 9, the Americans dropped a second atomic bomb, this time on the Japanese city of Nagasaki.

We began to hear that some prominent Japs had committed hari kari - killed themselves. We knew something had happened but we didn't know what. We still could not use the radio because it was a life sentence to have a radio or to listen to American music or American news. I was ordered by the Japs to help dig trenches. We asked them, "What are the trenches for?"

152

"When the Americans come, we hide in them." This was not true, because later we saw that they put machine guns on both ends of the trenches.

Then we heard about the bombs, and we eventually learned that the bombing of Hiroshima and Nagasaki saved my life and the lives of thousands of others. President Truman got the word - American Indians intercepted the code of the Japanese - that Hirohito had ordered the prison guards to kill all the prisoners within two weeks. So Truman couldn't wait. He gave the Japanese Emperor an ultimatum, "Surrender, or else!" Hirohito wouldn't do it, so Truman dropped the bombs. If it hadn't been for the bombs, it's likely we all could have been killed.

Finally, on August 15, 1945, Japan capitulated. U.S. President Harry Truman accepted the surrender and proclaimed the end of the war. On September 2, aboard the USS Missouri in Tokyo Bay the Japanese signed the formal surrender document.

It was reported later by the United Nations that, in addition to the casualties of armed conflict during the war, some four million people died in Indonesia due to famine, imprisonment, and forced labor.

That is how we got through the war.

41.

RESTLESS NATIVES

The war years produced a dramatic change in national attitudes and politics on the islands. On August 18, 1945, Sukarno, a native Indonesian, activist, and collaborator with the Japanese during the occupation, declared the independence of The Republic of Indonesia and himself as President. But the Dutch were still a force to be reckoned with and made a concerted effort to reassert their rule. This was the beginning of much countrywide struggle, bloodshed, and negotiations for Indonesia's future.

MG: When the war was over what did the Japanese do?

EF: The Japanese stayed on, but they were basically under the supervision of the Dutch. They became very meek. Lots of former Dutch prisoners took revenge and killed their captors.

With the war over and independence declared, many Indonesians began rioting. Instead of waiting for the allied forces, the Japanese allowed the natives to take possession of their arms. The weapons were used against the Dutch.

FF: The Indonesians were worse than the Japanese.

EF: Lots of the Indonesians were beautiful people. They were like substitute parents to us.

FF: Some of them.

EF: The younger ones, however - the half educated - were terrible. We called them pamudas. They first took out their anger against the Japs, who had been cruel to them, but then against the Dutch and other Europeans and their descendants.

FF: They didn't want the Dutch anymore. They came house to house, murdered the people, and stole what they could steal.

The natives rampaged through the streets of Jakarta and most of the towns on the islands of Java and Sumatra, killing thousands upon thousands of Europeans and their families, even babies. Heads and genitals were cut off, then tied together and thrown in the river.

EF: We heard a story of a mother with a baby. The mother's eyes were poked out and she was thrown in a well. Every house had a well for drinking water, sometimes twenty-five feet deep. The mother was thrown in the well, alive, and her baby was thrown in too. She couldn't see it, but she heard her baby drown.

The situation got real bad. We had no protection at all except for a few small weapons that I had managed to hide during the war. It seemed the allied forces would never come.

42.

BACK TO WORK

Just as quickly as their lives had been turned upside down at the start of the war, the denizens of Indonesia were propelled into another uncertain existence. Would the Dutch regain strength and dominance, or would the new, fledgling government take back what once belonged to the island natives?

As soon as the Japanese capitulated I was called back into service as Inspector of Police. I worked closely with the Dutch Army. I developed very good informers. One of them was Badaru, the same man who had brought me food and saved my life when I was in prison. (Sadly, I heard later that he was killed for helping me.)

**

I learned that a major mob attack - by the pamudas and the plopors, bad people who were against the Europeans and did everything to harm the Dutch - was going to take place in the middle of the night against Europeans in Jakarta. I turned in the report to my superior.

Usually my reports were taken 100% true. So, at six o'clock on the particular night that the attack was to take place, I rode my motorcycle past all the military posts. It turned out none of the posts had double forces. So I went to headquarters with a copy of my report. I said, "What happened to the extra guards?" I was told there were no extra guards. It turned out that for some reason, inconceivable to me, my superior had chosen to ignore my report. But upon my pressure and my urgency the posts were doubled. At exactly three o'clock that night the attack took place but it was repelled. Many, many people were likely saved because of my report.

**

Indonesians were killing European soldiers. Sometimes a soldier would be put on a plank over a pit and his throat cut with a sword. Then after three days his body was thrown in the river. Many bodies floated by. Then, to our surprise, Indonesian bodies started floating by, throats slashed in the same way. Since I spoke the language and knew the customs I was ordered by headquarters to look for the source and stop this procedure. I knew what was happening. Europeans whose family members had been dismembered or mutilated were getting their revenge. I and my men knew where it was happening, but we searched in other directions.

**

Every night around 2:00 a.m. I went out to catch killers. One night I was suddenly surrounded by about a dozen young males, nineteen to twenty-one years old. They said, "Can we go with you?"

I said, "What for?"

"We want to protect you."

I said, "I don't need your protection. I could call on the 10th Battalion Infantry if I need them."

They begged, "Oh, please can we go with you?" I felt so sorry for them because I knew their stories. I knew some of the guys' parents, how the parents suffered and were murdered by the Indonesians.

I said, "OK, but no funny stuff. You don't torture anybody, you don't kill anybody."

"Oh, we promise we won't do anything. We're just going to protect you."

The first person I caught that night was a witch doctor who had many murders to his name. He claimed he was immune to any attack, from anyone, with any object.

There was still time for another patrol so I told my "helpers" to stay put with my prisoner. I said, "I want him alive. I want him whole. Nothing is going to happen to him."

"Oh, no, we promise," they said solemnly.

But they knew the story of this witch doctor. My investigation later revealed that, when I was out of sight and hearing range, they asked the man if he was really a witch doctor and was he really immune to pain and harm. He defiantly proclaimed it to be true.

The boys had swords - Samurais - so sharp that one could shave with them. One young man pivoted his sword between two fingers and let it fall on the bare back of the prisoner. The sword made a big gash. The young man said to his friends, "Look how he is immune to any cutting!" Then hell broke loose. All the boys went berserk. They proceeded to cut the man to pieces. When I got back I found "hamburger", just a pile of meat, a bloody mess of cut-up bones and flesh. Headquarters called me on the carpet for that incident but apparently forgave me. I got out of it, I don't know how.

**

There were many, many more cases of cruelty. An Indonesian woman was married to a Dutchman. An old Indonesian man, over seventy, burned her to pieces with soldering irons. Her eyes were burned out, her ears were burned. It was terrible. When I got in that building, the smell was terrible. The old man didn't see anything wrong with it. "She was married to a Dutchman, so she had to be killed."

43.

A POLICEMAN'S INTUITION

Although Ernest was reluctant to reveal the details of most of his police activities, there is no doubt that he was very good at his job.

In November, 1945 Rika suffered from a pregnancy outside the uterus, so she had to go to a hospital. It was in an unprotected area with Indonesian doctors. They decided to use icepacks to stop the bleeding, but the nurses - who were Indonesian - did not do it. The problem got so bad that Rika went into a coma. An operation was urgent. But she needed blood and we had to find a donor. It was determined that my cousin, Ferry Cramer (he became a medical doctor after the war), had the same blood type and he agreed to donate. Blood was transferred directly from him to Rika in the hospital room.

When I visited Rika I found a man sitting in front of her room. Time after time he was there. I knew his intent. He was waiting for a time to strike. I told the doctor I wanted my wife taken to a protected area. He told me that transporting her would kill her for sure. I said, "I take responsibility. If she dies, I'd rather have her in one piece. I don't want to pick up her bones and legs and arms all over the country." So I had to sign in front of three doctors and Rika was transferred by ambulance to a small hospital in a protected area.

MFG: She was still in a coma?

EF: Yes. And that man and others - they were after her to punish me - must have thought, because of the ambulance transport, that Rika was in the operating room. They bombed that operating room. They killed the doctor, the nurses, and the lady on the operating table. Rika could have died in that attack, but fortunately she was recuperating on the other side of the building. After two weeks she got out of hospital and came home.

One night, though, while Riek was still in the hospital, I told Mam Luikens that I was not sleeping at home that night. I told her I had a premonition that something was going to happen to me if I stayed home. That night Indonesians came. They asked Jopie, "Where is the Nica dog?" – meaning me.

[NICA, Netherlands Indies Civil Administration, was a short-lived semi-military organization established to restore Dutch civil administration and law after the Japanese capitulation. The Indonesian revolutionaries were, of course, at odds with NICA's objectives.]

Fortunately I was not at home. They even looked up in the ceiling to check if I was there. If they had found me I would not be alive to write this.

44.

THE HOUSE ON STRUISWYKSTRAAT

When one thinks upon bygone days, certainly a few memories loom larger and are more immediately brought to mind. For Rika and Nes, and perhaps for many other Luikenses and Flissingers, the Luikens family home in Jakarta has always sparked vivid and passionate recollections. But the memories are all that remain.

Because I was a policeman and worked with the Dutch military, I had to be very cautious for myself and also for our family. The rioting and looting was getting closer to our neighborhood. Then one day the house next door was looted. It became obvious that the mobs were going to attack Mam Luikens's house, probably the next day. There wasn't much we could do. We couldn't shoot or do anything because it would have been against the law. The bastards could do what they wanted. But I was so apprehensive that I decided to give a hand grenade to each of Marie's sons, Wolter, twelve, and Boetie, thirteen. I told them, "If they try to break in, pull the pin and throw the grenade in the crowd."

I'm very glad it didn't go that far. Actually, I would have been a murderer because I had instigated it. Fortunately the mob did not come that next day, but we knew we had to go where it was safer. We all decided to evacuate the house.

MG: Where did you go?

FF: There were several protected areas. Nes, Maja, and I, and my sister, Marie, moved into one place. Mam Flissinger moved into another with a friend. My mother and Jopie and Marie's children stayed another day or so because there were so many things. They had to decide what to take because they couldn't take everything. Unfortunately the looters came while they were still there.

EF: Jopie tried to stand up to them but it was no use. The looters took almost everything.

FF: My mam and Jopie and the children left the next day and found a place in another protected area.

MG: Marie went with you, not with her children?

FF: Yes, she was there to help take care of Maja, because I had just come out of the hospital [still recovering from the extrinsic uterine pregnancy].

MG: In the protected areas who was protecting you?

EF: The Dutch military and the Gurkas – the British-Indian military.

MG: When did they come?

EF: Several months after the war was over.

MG: What brought them there?

EF: They were part of the allied forces. Then the Scottish came later. I have all praise for the Scottish guys. They were fantastic. If I reported a terrible murder, they took care of it on the spot. I cannot say that for the Americans or the Australians.

FF: The Australians were pretty good, though.

EF: But not as firm as the Scottish people. I have all praise for them.

Before long, that beautiful house on Struiswykstraat, like a palace, that Mam Luikens had bought when her husband died, was destroyed - broken down to the very last brick.

I must say this. Mam Luikens was, in my eyes, the personification of love and all that is good. When her husband died she received a large sum of money, a lump sum pension, from Shell. She bought the house on Struiswykstraat, free and clear, and had a good deal left to live on. It was a hard life raising six children, but they were brought up and educated very well.

Mam Luikens was a beautiful person with a fantastic attitude towards life. She was always cheerful and was always willing to help anybody whether it was financially or with advice. I loved her with all my heart. It is not easy to express myself about her whole being, because she was all that was decent, pleasant, loyal, and loving.

All these qualities and more I experienced more than once. She was fond of all her children and grandchildren and was an inspiration to all who came in contact with her.

While there was money, "friends" were constantly inviting themselves over to the Luikens house, in particular at meal times and on Sundays for a picnic or lunch. There was no Sunday without these "fair weather" friends. Some of them borrowed money and never returned it and vanished. Still, Mam Luikens was always cheerful and ready to help. She even hocked her jewelry to help others. Unfortunately, in most all cases, when she had the money to buy back the items, all she got back was junk. Instead of diamonds worth many thousands of dollars she got glass. And gold had been replaced by plated steel. This went on for years, and when the money was gone there were no friends, not one to help her in time of need. Yet, with all this cheating and stealing, Mam Luikens remained a beautiful person.

But the disloyalty and lying by so-called "friends" had a major effect on Rika. She observed it all and developed a very keen sense of human nature - and profound distrust. She has maintained an attitude of suspicion of other people her whole life. Can you blame her?

45.

POW'S

As with most wars the formal end does not bring an immediate return to normalcy. If only from a purely logistical standpoint, the inflictions of the Japanese occupation would take some time to be rectified.

EF: Even though the Japanese had surrendered, many people were still in prison camps. Ko had been released, but my father, who had been relocated to Tjimahi, West Java, was still in the camp there. I went there to bring him home. He was sitting in a chair in the camp yard and he called my name. I did not recognize him. He was so frail, a bag of bones, looking at me through bright, piercing eyes, tears running down his face. He couldn't stand. He cried like a kid. After some moments he regained his composure. But he was a broken man.

At the same time, it turned out, my mother, who had been living with a friend, had also decided to go to the prison to bring Pap home. Unbeknownst to her, we were already on our way back. Unfortunately she got stopped by the Indonesians and was held in detention for about a week. But then she was released. Finally my parents were reunited - for the first time in three years.

[Many years later, Maja, while looking through family papers, ran across a Dutch prayer. Ernest informed her that his father, while in prison, had prayed that prayer every day. It remains a treasured family heirloom (translation by Frederika):]

Houd nooit op, O God, Uw zegen over ons uit te storten.
> Never stop, O God, shedding Your blessings upon
> us.

Zend ons Uw Goddelyke bystand.
> Send us Your Godly support.

*Verlicht ons verstand met de stralen van Uw Goddelyke
licht.*
> Enlighten our understanding with Your divine
> light.

Versterk onze zwakheid.
> Strengthen our weaknesses.

Vervul onze harten met Uw liefde.
> Fill our hearts with Your love.

*Genees de bedorvenheid van onzen wil, opdat wy
overwinnen al het geweld van onze zichtbare en onze
onzichtbare vyanden.*
> Heal the corruption of our will, in order for us to
> overpower all the forces of our visible and our
> invisible enemies.

*God, mogen behagen, help ons voor het Heilig gebruik van
Uw genade.*
> God, if it pleases You, help us by the Holy use of
> Your grace.

Later Pap told me that young guys in his camp were nice to him, brought him food, and did his laundry. This was what I had hoped would happen and it materialized.

EF: Bert was released from his prison in Tokyo, too. There were times during his imprisonment that he had been brutally tortured. When he walked out of the prison, a Jap said something insulting to him. Bert was unable to restrain himself. He beat up on the Jap. That was actually a life sentence. They put him back in prison and tortured him again. And it turned out they poisoned his food. When the Americans came, it took six months to get the poison out of his system. Still filled with resentment, on the first day out of the allied forces hospital he took out his anger again on another Jap. Back into the hospital for another year! It was 1949 before I saw him again.

46.

FAMILY FORTUNES

After a number of months the Indonesian uprising and rioting subsided. Many of the Dutch in the protected areas moved back into houses that had not been destroyed but had been victimized and were no longer occupied. Frans and Martina Flissinger moved into one, Mrs. Luikens, Jopie, Marie and her children found another, and Ernest, Frederika, and Maja, another.

EF: As a policeman, an inspector, I took it upon myself, without the consent of my superiors, to go after the terrorists. I did it every night at two, three o'clock. I went out, with cash, and I paid my informants for information. One night one of them came to the house. He told Rika, "Tell your husband he better not cross the river tonight (where my territory was) or you and your daughter will be killed."

EF: I got the guy, the assassin, that same night. But it got me to thinking - what was going to happen to my family later on, because it was not going to get better.

****

On February 25, 1946, in Adelaide, South Australia, René and Rhonda gave birth to their first child, Susan Elizabeth Flissinger.

****

FF: Around March, 1946 Wolter, my brother, came home to Jakarta from prison camp in Singapore. He was sick. The doctors didn't know what he had. He died about a month later, on April 13. He was only thirty-six years old.

MG: He had been in prison camp for how long?

EF: Three and a half years. Such a good man.

****

In 1946 René, with Rhonda and infant Susan, returned to Jakarta where he joined the Royal Dutch Airlines, K.L.M., as a second pilot. René had to his credit, in the N.E. I. Air Force, forty-three raids in the Pacific for which he received the Flying Cross.

****

On September 28, 1946, in Jakarta, a second son, Roy Alfons Flissinger, was born to Ko and Leoni.

47.

A WHILE IN THE ISLES

It was certainly the hope that the former good times would return for everyone. But change is the real constant in life and, as much as some might wish, there is no going back. As a rule, though, most people make the necessary adjustments and forge ahead.

> *EF: Because of the possible kidnapping or murder of Maja and Rika, I was afraid for them. I was afraid of the torture we had seen during and after the war. So I asked for a transfer. Headquarters was eager to transfer me because they didn't like my attitude. I was very stern with the people. They were happy to transfer me to the remotest part of Indonesia, to the island of Ambon, west of New Guinea. Maja was then almost a year old.*

Soon after arriving in Ambon, however, Nes received another transfer, to a tiny island, Kisar, just off the eastern tip of East Timor. The threesome resided there for about eight months before Nes was recalled to Ambon.

On December 19, 1946, in Ambon, Rika gave birth to a son, Raymond Ernest Everhard Flissinger.

> *MG: What was it like – your living situation there?*

> *FF: There was nothing to complain about while*

we were there on the little islands. We always had a house and servants to help with the children. After Ray was born we moved to another small island, Banda Neira, for about eight months, then back again to Ambon.

Because there were servants to help with daily living and tend to the children, Frederika was able to restart her teaching career. Even though the family moved about the islands for several years, she found her services were needed wherever they went.

**

In the spring of 1947 Ernest, in his capacity as policeman, encountered an automobile-bicycle collision in Ambon involving a Mr. John Tinsman, an American missionary with the Assembly of God Church. As one of the few English-speaking people in the area, Ernest was able to "untangle" the incident. Following this, Ernest and John struck up a brief friendship until Tinsman returned to America. Who could have foreseen that this chance meeting would have such a significant impact on the future of the Flissinger family. For the first time Ernest and Frederika began thinking of possibly emigrating out of Indonesia.

****

Bert, having survived the terrible hardships of the

Japanese prison camps but still in the Dutch Navy Air Service, was in Surabaya when he met and married Clara Olivia (Ollie) Carter on April 3, 1947. Ollie had been born in that city, November 14, 1927.

✳✳✳✳

[From René's autobiographical writings:]
"In 1947 I received a special course for three months on the Mitchell bomber and then was posted back to the Air Force 18th Squadron in Jakarta."

✳✳

EF: My brother, René, came for a visit in Ambon in 1947. It was so good to see him. He asked me to take a walk along the beach. He wanted to see what it looked like. During the war one of his bombing missions was against the Japanese occupying Ambon. Fortunately the beauty of the island had not been destroyed.

✳✳✳✳

On November 5, 1947, in Jakarta, Ko and Leoni begot son number three, Marcel Frank Flissinger.

✳✳✳✳

On November 22, 1947, Anthony René Flissinger was

born in Jakarta. He was the second child and first son for René and Rhonda. Shortly thereafter, in January, 1948 René went to work for Veem Combination in Jakarta as an auto mechanic. Then in June of that year he began working for the Department of Shipping (Scheepvaart) with the rank of Overseer of 1st Class, involved with overseeing lighthouses.

$$****$$

Back in Ambon, a second son, Bartholomeus (Barry) Sylvester Flissinger, was born to Nes and Rika on December 14, 1948.

$$****$$

About this time Jopie came to live with Rika and Nes. She had joined the Dutch military after the war, and while she was stationed in New Guinea a relationship developed that resulted in a pregnancy. On March 14, 1949 (on Maja's fourth birthday!), Jopie gave birth to a son, Peter Luikens.

$$****$$

My job on the islands was to capture Japanese war criminals, which I did. But it turned out there was more I had to deal with in these remote outposts. There was corruption of some people higher up in the Dutch forces.

There was the case of the CARE packages.

Some officers were stealing these provisions from the poor people. I decided to look into it. I investigated the low man and the middle man. Then I went to the magistrate, my superior. I asked, "What do you think? Shall I go on?"

He said, "It's up to you."

I said, "Yes, I want to. I want to investigate the colonel, the lieutenant colonel, and the rest of them."

He seemed anxious. "This is rough ground."

I said, "Yes, but it's unfair. Why should I get the middle man only?" I asked permission to investigate the next guy.

I had coffee and dinner at the perpetrator's house. Then I turned in a report. The very next day I had a telegram from headquarters. It read, "Quit the case. Abandon the case."

I went to the magistrate and asked him, "What do you think?"

He said, "Well, it's up to you. You have it in your hands."

I wired headquarters, "No chance. Too far advanced."

Back came a more emphatic command, "Drop it - or else!"

My response was, "What is the 'or else'?"

The final telegram was a transfer out of Ambon, assigning me again to the police academy - with a promotion to the rank of commissioner.

48.

DIVERGING DESTINIES

With a new rank and a family of five, Ernest moved back to Sukabumi in 1949 and continued his police service. Frederika found a teaching position there as well. Jopie, with infant Peter, moved back to Jakarta to live again with her mother.

MG: How was your life in Sukabumi, with the three children?

FF: It was pretty much the same as other places we lived. We had a house, in the area where a lot of other police were housed. And we had servants. We had brought a nanny – another woman named Marie – with us from Ambon.

That same year Ernest received a surprise communication. John Tinsman wrote to say that John's father, a minister in Redding, California, had agreed to sponsor Ernest, Frederika, and the three children in their efforts to move to America. The paperwork had been started. The Flissingers were now on a waiting list for U. S. immigration! However, no one had any idea how long the wait might be.

It was also in 1949 that Ernest reconnected with his brother, Bert, who was by then out of the Navy Air Service and working for a company called Lindetevis in its department of currency. On April 20, in Surabaya, Bert and Ollie had given birth to their first child, Roland Harald Flissinger. In addition to the long overdue reunion of siblings, the meeting was the first for the wives and children.

MG: And you hadn't seen Bert for how long?

FF: Since the war started, in 1942.

✳✳✳✳

In March, 1949 René, now with the rank of Head-overseer, was posted to the city of Makassar, the capital of South Sulawesi (Island), Indonesia. He was in charge of the lighthouses on the surrounding islands. He relocated his family with him, and on October 2, 1949, he and Rhonda welcomed their third child, Sandra Martina Flissinger.

****

June 12, 1949 brought a fourth son, Dennis Jacobus Flissinger, to Ko and Leoni in Jakarta.

****

In December, 1949 The Netherlands, after four years of post-war conflict and under heavy international pressure, formally recognized the independence of the Republic of Indonesia. The new Republic established a two-year window for "foreigners" - most definitely including all the Dutch - living in Indonesia. By the end of 1951, each would be required either to accept Indonesian citizenship, remain as a foreigner, or leave the country. In the meantime, Ernest, as commissioner of police, was "loaned out" to the new Republic.

****

In September, 1950 René moved his family back to Jakarta because he had been reposted there.

****

Earned furloughs were still being provided, and in March of 1951 Nes, Rika, and the children prepared and packed for a trip to The Netherlands. But in another turn of events the plans changed. Word came that their names had come to the top of the U.S. immigration list. Before the year's end, the young Flissinger family would be pulling up their native roots and replanting in more fertile soil.

> *EF: Before we left my father said to me, "Why do you go to America? You're not going to have a chance."*
>
> *I said, "Pap, we've got to do something. We cannot stay here."*
>
> *MG: Why did he think you wouldn't have a chance in America?*
>
> *FF: Because he knew about the Negroes in America at that time* [anti-Negro civil rights events].
>
> *MG: He was afraid of discrimination against you?*
>
> *FF: Probably.*

But he didn't suffer the angst for very long. On June 8, 1951, Frans Willem Flissinger passed away in Jakarta. It was on his sixty-third birthday.

MJG: And I remember we were in Sukabumi when he died.

FF: Yes. I remember I was in the back yard taking care of orchids and I got an intuition.

MG: An intuition?

FF: Yes. And I said, "Somebody died." But I didn't know who. Then Pap got a telephone call that his father had died.

MFG: I remember that day. Pop said Opa died in his sleep. Pop was crying. Outside he put on his hat. Then he got on his motorcycle and left. I remember.

**

When Ernest learned that he and his family would at last be emigrating to the United States, he asked his eighteen-year-old nephew, Wolter van der Torren, if he might also be interested in coming to America. Even though there would be a long waiting period, Wolter agreed to have his name put on the U.S. immigration list.

****

On July 8, 1951, in Jakarta, Jennifer Ann Flissinger was born, the fourth child for René and Rhonda.

****

Also in 1951 Ko and Leoni, with their four sons, emigrated to Australia, finding residence in Bullaburra, New South Wales. This small town in the Blue Mountains west of Sydney was an allocated refugee location for Dutch displaced from Indonesia. Before too long the family moved to nearby Valley Heights, selected for its cheap land and proximity to a railway station. Ko took up the career of train driver.

****

That same year Marie van der Torren Luikens, widow of Rika's brother, Wolter, emigrated to The Netherlands with her two sons, Han and Wolter.

49.

THE NEW WORLD

After a short farewell visit with family in Jakarta, Ernest and Frederika and their three children, Maja, Ray, and Barry, boarded the Norwegian freighter, MS FERNBAY, bound for America. It was December 14, 1951.

MG: How were arrangements made for the trip?

FF: When we were ready to leave, there was only one ship, the FERNBAY, leaving from Jakarta going all the way to America. It had only four passenger cabins, but they were very nice.

MG: *What do you remember about that trip? You went from Jakarta to...*

FF: *First to Cheribon, another little city away from Jakarta, and then we went to Ceylon where I remember meeting up with René.*

MJG: *(remembering) Ceylon, with the big elephants.*

MG: *How did you know René was there?*

FF: *Well, his wife was still in Jakarta.*

MG: *So, from Rhonda you learned that René was in Ceylon. And you went to meet him.*

FF: *No, he came on board the ship, just for a short visit while we were in port there. Then we went through the Suez Canal to the Mediterranean.*

MG: *Were there any stops there?*

FF: *There were stops, because there was another family traveling – I think they were Jews or Israelites. And then we crossed the Atlantic to Boston. We stayed there a couple of days before the ship went on to New York City.*

Ray remembers disembarking in Boston at the age of five. It was snowing. The gangplank was quite slippery and he lost his footing. If it had not been for his father's quick hands, he would have ended up in Massachusetts Bay.

The MS FERNBAY arrived in New York City Harbor

in January, 1952, passing, as most ships do there, the Statue of Liberty.

MG: And how long were you in New York?

FF: I believe about ten days, maybe two weeks.

MG: Was that by choice or were you waiting for something?

FF: We had orchid plants I had brought with us and we had to wait till we got permission to take the orchids.

MJG: How many did you have, about twenty?

FF: No, not that many, just a few that were special.

MG: Did you know that you were going to have to wait?

FF: No, not before they told us.

MJG: Were there purple ones? And white ones?

FF: Yes, white ones, too.

MJG: That's why I had orchids in my wedding bouquet, because you had brought orchids from Indonesia.

Immigration records state the Flissingers entered the country on January 30, 1952. This appears to be the official date they were admitted after waiting for clearance due to bringing the orchids with them.

FF: Then we took a train to Chicago and on to California.

The three-day train ride brought them to Sacramento, California on February 8, 1952. They were met by John Tinsman who took them to their final destination in the nearby town of Woodland. The immigrants were at last free of the anxieties and tribulations of a turbulent homeland and they were about to embark on a new life journey.

But Nes and Rika had no idea what the future would hold. The family arrived in California with thirty dollars to their name.

MG: You ended up in Sacramento with very little money, but you were expecting the Dutch to...

FF: Pay Pap a pension. That was the only way we could afford to come to America.

MG: We think of a pension as after one retires. Why was The Netherlands paying Pop a pension at that time?

FF: Well, we didn't call it a pension at that time. How do you call it...?

MG: Benefits?

FF: Yes.

MG: So they were compensating Pop for the years he worked in Indonesia.

FF: Yes.

MG: And that started soon after you got here?

FF: Yes. But the first month we didn't have that money. We borrowed money for a month from a man we met here. He was from Holland. He worked for a bank in San Francisco. Pap asked him if he could loan us some money for a month for rent, maybe five hundred dollars, and he loaned us the money. Then at the end of the month the money came from Holland so we were able to pay back the loan.

MG: And the Dutch have been paying that money ever since.

FF: Yes, regularly.

MG: How very fortunate.

FF: Yes, but it would have been better if they had paid me too.

MG: You never got anything for the years you worked there?

FF: No. They claimed I only had eleven years in, so I couldn't get it. So Pap was the only one that got paid.

[It appears that back then a minimum of twelve years of government service was required for an employee to receive benefits/pension from The Netherlands. Because of the war the pension administration compensated each employee by adding three years to each one's length of service. This meant that Nes qualified, barely. Rika,

187

however, even with the added three years, was disappointingly short by one year.]

**

It is probable that the Flissingers were the first Indo-Europeans to immigrate to the Sacramento area following the war. As a result of this distinction the local Woodland newspaper made a point to interview the aspiring U.S. citizens. A few weeks later a similar article appeared in The Sacramento Bee.

WOODLAND DEMOCRAT   FEBRUARY 11, 1952

Weary of Strife

Indo-Europeans Seek Work, Peace Here

A self-exiled Indo-European without a country brought his family to Woodland three days ago to look for work and make a home.

"We want to have peace for the first time in ten years, to give our children an education and a future. We are really glad to be out of Indonesia now," E. H. Flissinger

188

said yesterday, speaking for his wife and three children.

The former inspector of police in Indonesia was able to bring his family to America through the sponsorship of Mr. and Mrs. John Tinsman, Assembly of God missionaries who are staying in Woodland pending their return to Indonesia in March.

Flissinger explained his fateful meeting with Tinsman in Indonesia in the spring of 1947, when, as an English speaking police officer, he was able to untangle an auto-bicycle collision in which Tinsman had become involved.

The favor was soon returned when Tinsman helped his official friend get on a United States immigration list. The family had to wait nearly three years before boarding the Norwegian vessel that brought them halfway around the world to California and the Tinsmans.

"We have much to learn in this country," Flissinger said. "I will try to find a mechanic's job to use my hands now, because my university education and police training is very different from American methods."

Making the trip by way of the Suez, the Mediterranean and across the Atlantic to

Boston, the Flissingers agreed that their first impression of America was the kindness with which they were treated.

"We hadn't received such kindness for several years, and people of Boston told us that the people of California would be even more friendly, which is true." Flissinger said smiling.

"We were astonished at the greatness of the country when we first landed and were impressed with the rapid speed of life we saw in New York," injected Mrs. Flissinger.

The former police commissioner said he hadn't seen so much snow since he was in Holland in 1929.

The Flissinger's three children, Maja, 6; Ray, 5; and Barry, 3; are just beginning to pick up a few words of English.

Mrs. Flissinger has been launched on a course in how to prepare American dishes by Mrs. Tinsman and Mrs. Richard Fulmer. As in most of Asia, rice is the basic staple in the Indonesian diet and menu. Mrs. Flissinger was baffled by "strange American foods called marshmallows, Jell-O and shortening."

Like all Indo-Europeans, the Flissingers fell out of favor when the former Dutch colony became the Indonesian Republic in

December 1949, under the piloting of Java president Sukarno.

The Flissingers, a mixture of Dutch, Indonesian and French, were given two years either to accept Indonesian citizenship, remain foreigners, or leave their native country.

Flissinger estimated that less than 1% of the Indo-Europeans have accepted citizenship in the Republic and that thousands have already immigrated to Australia and New Zealand where entry quotas are less stringent than in the United States.

The Southeast Asian archipelago has been in a state of ferment and upheaval since the Japanese capitulated, Flissinger said. Guerrilla warfare has been carried on by island subjects who refused to accept the leadership of the Javanese who have been instrumental in setting up the Republic.

According to Flissinger, the inhabitants of the different island groups differ in language, culture and religion. The islands of Sumatra, Celebes and Molucca are in open revolt against the Javanese who controlled the Republic at present.

The Dutch were not able to reestablish their colonial ties with the island group following the war, so as a civil servant of the Dutch government, Flissinger has been on loan to the Indonesian government for the past two years as police commissioner.

The island family believe that the standard of living will not regain its prewar level under native rule. They conceded that the Dutch may have exploited the people economically, but the subjects were "not suppressed."

Mrs. Frederika Flissinger, a former grammar school teacher who was discharged by the Republican government because she spoke only island Dutch, was responsible for freeing her husband when he was imprisoned by the Japanese in Batavia during the war.

Flissinger said that there have been three attempts made on his family by the Indonesian government in its policy to rid the island of Dutch-trained policeman and Army personnel.

In reviewing first impressions of America, the couple admitted that they were amazed at the trusting nature of newspaper owners who leave their products on the streets and trust the public, not only to pay for the papers, but to leave the racks intact.

It would be impossible to leave items

unattended on the streets of Indonesia, Flissinger said.

The couple explained that the newspaper example typified a security, trust and internal peace that they had come west - halfway around the world - to find.

FROM INDONESIA - Pictured above is the Flissinger family who came to Woodland from Indonesia three days ago. From left to right are Maja, 6, Mrs. Frederika Flissinger, Ray, 5, E.H. Flissinger, and Barry, 3. Ray is holding a hand-carved Sawoh wood-head from Bali.

**

Although it was John Tinsman's father, living in Redding, California, who actually sponsored the Flissingers, arrangements were made for the new immigrants to first have an apartment in Woodland, the small farming community just northwest of Sacramento where John and his family lived. But within a week or so, by way of a notice placed with the Assembly of God Church in Woodland, a job opportunity came Ernest's way. A church member, Roy Shurrum, who owned a ranch in the small town of Freeport just south of Sacramento, was in need of help. He hired Ernest as a ranch hand and the Flissingers went to live on the ranch.

> *MG: So, when you left Indonesia, you knew you had a place to stay but you didn't know...*
>
> *FF: About the job, no.*

The novice ranch hand's duties included tending to cattle and pigs and rabbits and chickens, milking cows, cleaning stables, mowing and bailing and stacking hay, helping with cattle auctions, various other routine ranching and maintenance chores, and even some bookkeeping. Ernest worked fourteen to twenty hours a day.

**

A few days after the family arrived at Shurrum Ranch there was a severe storm. After it had passed, three-year-old Barry was playing in one of the outbuildings. The big door to the building fell inward off its hinges, crashing down, striking the boy. If it had not also landed on an inflated tire tube and a truck tire, the youngster might have been killed.

But he was injured. An employee of the ranch rushed Nes, Rika, and Barry to the nearest hospital a few miles away. Barry's leg and collarbone were broken. Nes, who needed to stay on the job, went back to the ranch with the other worker while a doctor tended to the injuries. With Barry's arm in a sling and his leg in a cast, Rika had little choice but to walk home carrying her son. It must have been quite an ordeal. Fortunately a policeman saw Rika's struggle and took the mother and child the last part of the way in his patrol car, displaying another fine example of the American goodwill Rika and Ernest were learning to appreciate.

**

MG: In 1952, when you went to the ranch, Maja was old enough to go to school.

FF: Yes, in Freeport.

MG: She showed me the building, a very small, perhaps two-room schoolhouse. It was there in Freeport until it was razed only a few years ago.

FF: Yes, she went into the first grade there.

**

Per U.S. immigration law, Ernest and Frederika would have to establish five years of residency in America, have a reasonable command of the English language, and pass a test regarding basic American history and government before applying for U.S. citizenship. The children, if still under eighteen would automatically become citizens when both the parents were naturalized.

✳✳✳✳

On May 16, 1952, back in Jakarta, Bert and Ollie welcomed their second son, Jeffrey Roger Flissinger.

✳✳✳✳

Life on the ranch was working out fine for Nes and family. But luck took a turn.

> FF: We stayed at the ranch until the end of the year. Then they fired Pap because he had an accident. He broke his right elbow and couldn't work. Shurrum said, "I cannot use you if you cannot work anymore." So we had to leave the ranch. We had three cows. We had to leave them.
>
> MG: You owned three cows?
>
> FF: Yes. Pap had bought three calves, but we couldn't take them with us.
> Then Pap went to a priest in south Sacramento and the priest sent him to Mr. Roger Slakey, co-owner of Slakey Brothers [a distributor of heating, air conditioning, and plumbing supplies]. And Slakey said to Pap, "Can

you read, can you write?" and Pap said yes.

MG: Mr. Slakey was in that parish where the priest was?

FF: No, I think the priest knew him. He was a very, very Catholic man, Mr. Slakey. But he couldn't hire Pap right away because Pap wasn't in the union, so Mr. Slakey knew a guy who owned a gas station and he asked the guy to hire Pap and he did.

MG: The gas station was located where?

FF: It was downtown somewhere? It must have been K Street.

MG: How long did Pop work there?

FF: Not that long. Maybe a few weeks, then he got hired by Slakey.

MG: He was able to get into the union that fast?

FF: Yes.

Local 447A was a plumbers union. Not all but some of the Slakey business involved plumbing supplies. Ernest, with no background in plumbing, had to be "recommended" by another union member. Mr. Slakey arranged for this to happen and once Ernest's membership was on the books, Slakey hired him, February 1, 1953.

All new hires at Slakey worked their way up the ranks, learning every aspect of the business and the products.

Ernie, as he came to be called there, followed his predecessors through the departments of receiving, order filling, shipping, and "inside" sales.

50.

A PIECE OF

THE AMERICAN DREAM

Despite the turn of events at Shurrum Ranch, Ernest and Frederika had managed their finances well enough to mortgage a home for their family. On January 31, 1953, they rented and moved into a house at 2658 Gary Way in North Sacramento. Two months later, on March 30, they became legal owners of the house.

[North Sacramento was an incorporated city from 1925 to 1964, surrounded by and within the boundaries of the city of Sacramento. In 1964 North Sacramento was annexed into Sacramento. As occasionally happens in growing urban areas, two streets in Sacramento bore the same name, Gary Way, and even some of the house numbers coincided. The city's solution to the matter was to renumber some of the residences. This resulted in the Flissingers' address being officially changed from 2658 to 2750.]

****

In February, 1954 René and Rhonda, with their son, three daughters, and also Martina Flissinger (now Oma to her family), emigrated to Australia. They settled in

199

Ivanhoe, New South Wales. René reestablished himself as an auto mechanic.

Ivanhoe, a small town "in the middle of nowhere" about five hundred miles west of Sydney seemed an odd choice, but Rhonda had good cause. Her parents had separated and her father was residing there. She thought it would be a good idea to be near him.

But that part of the country was extremely hot and Oma Flissinger was unable to tolerate it. Accepting an invitation from Ko, she found it more comfortable to live in Valley Heights with her son and Leoni who had been there since 1951.

> *MG: Did you see your mother again?*
>
> *EF: No, I never saw her again. I'm grateful to Ko for taking care of her.*

**

A fifth child, Gregory Brenton Flissinger, was born to René and Rhonda on April 25, 1954, in Broken Hill [where the nearest hospital was, about 200 miles west of Ivanhoe], New South Wales.

On June 15, 1954, in North Sacramento, Ernest and Frederika welcomed into the world their fourth child, Francis (Frank) John Flissinger, the first of this long line of Flissingers to be born in America.

51.

REUNITED

At the age of sixty-three, Martina Jacoba Adriana Broens Flissinger passed away on April 13, 1956, in Valley Heights, New South Wales, Australia.

EF: I remember it was Friday the 13th. That same day I squashed my left hand at Slakey Brothers. A big piece of metal fell on my hand. I was at work when I got the call about my mam.

MG: Had you been able to stay in contact with her?

EF: While she was there in Australia I could write to her. But my mother was not well educated. She could not write much.

A few years later Ko was able to retrieve Frans Flissinger's remains from Jakarta and Frans was respectfully reburied beside Martina in fitting recognition and celebration of their forty-two-year marriage.

****

On May 12, 1956, a third son, Reginald Gilbert Flissinger, was born to Bert and Ollie in Jakarta.

52.

BUILDING A NEST EGG

With Ernest well established at Slakey Brothers and the older children in school, time presented itself to enhance the family income. When a Gary Way neighbor was contracted to watch little Frank, Frederika, after a very brief stab at selling dresses door to door, stepped out into the labor force.

> *FF: I first got a job at a cannery on Richards Boulevard, choosing and separating good fruits and vegetables from bad. I think for just a month. And then I got a job at a laundry.*
>
> *MG: Were you doing the washing?*
>
> *FF: Not actually washing the clothes, but I would send them out. I worked there for about six months, but I guess they didn't think I was doing such a good job. So then I went to work at Golden State Linen on S Street downtown Sacramento. I worked there quite a while, three or four years.*
>
> *MG: What kind of work did you do?*
>
> *FF: I worked in the office. The drivers had to go out to addresses with the stuff. I had the addresses for them.*

53.

THE ULTIMATUM

The government of the young Republic of Indonesia, in spite of internal conflicts, was holding its own and learning what it would take to build the country into what their founders envisioned. As there was no love lost for the disenfranchised Indo-Europeans, the earlier proclamation was stiffened essentially to require: either apply for and accept Indonesian citizenship or get out! Life-altering choices had to be made by many people.

In 1945, in Jakarta, Sonja van der Torren had met Freddy Oscar Hommerson, born August 6, 1923, in Sukabumi. They had wed in Jakarta on July 9, 1947, and they had five children - Huibert, Robert, Willy, Andre, and Erica, all born in Jakarta - when, in the early 1950s, they emigrated to The Netherlands. Freddy, a school teacher in Jakarta, had for some time requested his salary be paid partly in local currency and partly in Dutch currency. As a result he and his family were financially more secure when they arrived in The Netherlands. (As the years passed they had two more children, Ilona and Maureen, both born in Dieren, The Netherlands.)

Boetie van der Torren, having become a merchant marine, had married a Chinese woman named Tan Ahwa and they had a daughter, Jeanne (fondly called Swaantje).

Wolter van der Torren, at age twenty-two, married Nora Andersen, twenty, in a church in Jakarta on July 22, 1956. The two had met in the capital city two years earlier when they were both working for Kolf & Company, a printer of, among other things, currency and stamps.

Later that same year, in Jakarta, the mother of these van der Torrens - Rika's sister, Marie, widowed fourteen years - married, on December 22, 1958, a man who was an acquaintance of her daughter, Sonja. His name was Johannus (Han) Albertus Klein, ten years Marie's junior, born September 9, 1917, in Surabaya. Sonja had introduced Han to Marie two years earlier.

By 1957 Bert Flissinger, like his brother, Nes, was finding it too dangerous to keep his family in Indonesia. That year he chose, with Ollie and their three boys, to emigrate to The Netherlands.

1958 brought the last vestiges of the Luikens family to a decision. In mid-January, on the MS WILLEM RUYS, Mam Luikens, Jopie with son, Peter, and Wolter and Nora van der Torren with newborn son, Gerome Maria van der Torren, born in Jakarta, December 8, 1957, were among the many who bid farewell to Indonesia with no earthly idea what their fortunes would bring in Europe. After passing through the Suez Canal the ship encountered a severe storm in the Mediterranean Sea. Almost everyone, including the captain, suffered seasickness. To make matters worse, another nearby ship was in distress, and, per maritime rules, any ships within reasonable distance to provide aid were obliged to do so. For three turbulent days the WILLEM

RUYS lent its support. After the crisis was resolved, the WILLEM RUYS continued its three-week voyage to The Netherlands.

[An historical note: The MS WILLEM RUYS, whose maiden voyage was in 1947, sailed under Dutch registry until 1965 when she was sold to an Italian company. After being renamed ACHILLE LAURO, the vessel became infamous when it was hijacked in 1985 by the Palestine Liberation Front. Cruising continued until late 1994 when, on one of its voyages, the engines caught fire. The ship had to be abandoned and she sank off the coast of Somalia after forty-seven years of service.]

A different decision was made by Han Klein. He was positioned in Java with a very good job and chose to become an Indonesian citizen. But he soon came to realize that most such naturalized Indo-Europeans were never going to be fully accepted by the natives. Disenchanted with the situation, Han and Marie also emigrated to The Netherlands in 1958.

Another family member who chose to take Indonesian citizenship was Sister Alexia. As her whole adult life had been dedicated to teaching and aiding those who lived in the Jakarta area, it was a logical decision.

The following year Boetie, with his wife and infant daughter emigrated to The Netherlands as well. But for Boetie it was not an easy move. He had contracted TB and had to make the voyage on a hospital ship. Fortunately, after extensive care from doctors in The Netherlands, he recovered, (and his family eventually grew there in The

Netherlands to include four more children, Wim, Jan, Maria, and Wolter).

$$**$$

The Dutch homeland was hardly prepared for the influx of the tens of thousands of Dutch-Indonesian expatriates. Very little housing was available. The relocated travelers were assigned to various small apartments or to shared quarters in homes. And these displaced "colonials" were not warmly accepted by the locals or readily acknowledged for all they had suffered.

$$****$$

In De Bilt, The Netherlands, Bert and Ollie's family expanded once more with the birth of their fourth boy, Frans Rudolf Flissinger on September 22, 1958.

54.

THE PLEDGE OF ALLEGIANCE

With the mandatory five years of residency requirement fulfilled, Ernest Hubert Flissinger applied and took the tests for U.S. citizenship. He was proudly sworn in on August 4, 1958.

Rika, however, just beginning to feel comfortable in the workplace, was not quite ready to conquer the exams. But on March 16, 1959, after satisfying all requisites, Frederika Adriana Flissinger was also sworn in as an American citizen.

At the same ceremony the children, Marguerite Jacqueline Flissinger, Raymond Ernest Everhard Flissinger, and Bartholomeus Sylvester Flissinger, all still under eighteen years of age and therefore eligible to be automatically naturalized when the second parent was sworn in, also took the oath. (Son Frank, by reason of his birth in the U.S., was already a citizen.)

55.

PAYING IT FORWARD

In the spring of 1960 Wolter and Nora van der Torren, living in Velp, The Netherlands, received word from U.S. Immigration that, if they still desired, they could come to America. As it was with Ernest and Frederika back in 1951, the requirements were that an immigrant must be sponsored by a U.S. citizen. The immigrant must also provide evidence in writing that he would have a place to live and employment when he got there.

Wolter contacted Ernest in Sacramento with his decision to make the move. Ernest and Frederika were delighted to serve as sponsors and provide housing for their nephew and family! To complete the matter, Ernest inquired of his boss, Mr. Slakey, if there might be a job opportunity for Wolter at Slakey Brothers. Mr. Slakey came through again. He provided a letter guaranteeing a job for Wolter upon his arrival.

In July Wolter, Nora, their firstborn, Gerome, and their second son, Glenn Franciscus van der Torren, born November 10, 1958, in Velp, The Netherlands, boarded in Rotterdam a passenger ship which, after a stop in South Hampton, England, made its way across the Atlantic to New York City. The vessel was much smaller and slower than the MS WILLEM RUYS which had carried them to The Netherlands. In fact, during the nine-day voyage they were passed twice by the SS United States, first on its way to Europe and again on its way back to America.

Then, like the Flissingers eight years earlier, the van der Torrens took a train from New York, via Chicago, to Sacramento and to a new life. For the first six months they resided in the Flissinger home before moving into a residence of their own.

∗∗∗∗

Also in 1960 René, Rhonda, and family moved to St. Marys, New South Wales, just west of Sydney, Australia.

∗∗∗∗

One can imagine that Bert Flissinger, raised alongside five brothers and being the father of four sons, must have been quite elated when Ollie gave birth to their daughter, Patricia Carmen Concita Flissinger, on January 23, 1962, in Utrecht, The Netherlands.

56.

THE MARCH OF TIMES

After almost a decade in the United States the Flissingers had comfortably secured themselves a place in the American pursuit of happiness.

> *FF: After I got my citizenship the girls at Golden State Linen asked me, "Why don't you try to work for the state?" So I took some tests, passed, and got hired at the State of California EDD (Employment Development Department.), 8th and Capitol Streets., as a computer programmer and analyst.*

✳✳✳✳

On February 16, 1966, eighty-three-year-old Marie Jacqueline de la Fonteyne Luikens passed away in Nymegen, The Netherlands.

Typical of her kind and generous nature, Oma Luikens was in her kitchen at the time baking a cake to ship to her granddaughter, Maja, in America, for Maja's twenty-first birthday.

Upon hearing of the passing, Sister Alexia back in Indonesia took a new name - Sister Jacqueline - in honor of her beloved mother.

****

By 1967 Ernest had been working for Slakey Brothers for fourteen years. He had proven himself to be a dedicated employee, climbing the ladder to a prominent position in inside sales. Due to the unfortunate passing of an outside salesman, Ernest was promoted to the resulting vacancy. He was able to use his naturally friendly and gregarious personality to become even more productive and successful for himself and for the company, travelling daily through his territory in the foothills east of Sacramento.

Within a few years Ernest was making substantially more income. With concerns about the decline of their residential neighborhood and also knowing they would soon have an "empty nest", Ernest and Frederika began looking to upgrade their living situation. On September 15, 1972, the couple purchased and moved into a house at 1921 Jamestown Drive in Sacramento. The Gary Way house was retained as rental property.

In the years that followed Ernest and Frederika invested in other pieces of property with an acute eye for future profits and also for vacation venues for the whole family. Over time their efforts were substantially rewarded.

****

1971 brought the retirement of Sister Jacqueline. She had been a nun and teacher for forty-four years, serving not only in Jakarta but in Surabaya, Flores Island, and Bandung. On April 12, she emigrated to The Netherlands. Though retired from her teaching duties, she remained committed to her religious vows and her life as a nun. She was also happy to be near her family again. For some reason, however - perhaps because she had taken Indonesian citizenship and there were still strained relations between The Netherlands and Indonesia - a laborious nine-year effort followed to regain her Dutch citizenship. Her sister, Jopie, even had to write a letter to Queen Juliana before the naturalization was finally granted.

****

In early summer, 1976 Ernest received word that his brother, René Adolf Flissinger, had passed away on June 11 in St. Marys, New South Wales, Australia.

****

Wolter and Nora van der Torren did not feel any urgency to become American citizens as quickly as Ernest and Frederika. It was not a requirement for U.S. residency or employment as long as they renewed their green cards. But on July 4, 1976, America's 200th birthday, they, along with sons Gerome and Glenn, were sworn in as citizens of the United States. (Their other two children, Fleurette Thresia van der Torren and Wolter John van der Torren, were born in the U.S.)

****

In 1978, after seventeen years with the state, Frederika retired at the age of sixty-two.

****

On December 19, 1980, in Nymegen, The Netherlands, Johannus (Han) Albertus Klein passed away at age sixty-three.

****

In 1982, at age sixty-five, Ernest retired from Slakey

Brothers after 29 years with the company. In the years that followed he rekindled his passion for knowledge in medicine and alternative healing methods. He read abundantly and kept extensive notes on these subjects, and he became quite proficient in the practice of reflexology.

****

René's wife, Rhonda, by 1982 widowed for six years, moved to Penrith, another suburb of Sydney, Australia.

****

At some point, the date undetermined, Tan Ahwa, Boetie's wife passed away. Subsequently, while on a visit to the country of his birth, a place that always tugged at his heart, Boetie met Eugenie Martens. They married and Eugenie took up residence with her husband in The Netherlands.

57.

RECONNECTIONS

By the 1980s the Flissinger and Luikens families had been spread to far corners of the world for some thirty years.

MG: After you came to America, did you know where all your relatives were, where they had moved?

FF: Yes, I wrote them letters.

MG: When they all emigrated to other countries, did you know they had left Indonesia.

FF: No, not until they got where they were going.

MG: And after they all got settled in these various places, who ever came to visit you here?

FF: Marie and Han came. And Moes came with them.

MG: And on Pop's side, did anyone come to visit here?

FF: Bert and Ollie and two of their children came over. Rhonda came once, maybe twice, with some of her children and grandchildren. Ko came over a couple times.

MG: With Leoni?

FF: No, by himself. Later on Leoni and her sister came over.

MG: Did your mom ever come?

FF: No, she never did. She wanted to, but she never had the money.

MG: Did you ever go to Holland?

FF: Yes, we went to Holland, with Frank, I think when Frank was ten or eleven. We saw my mam and Marie and Jopie and the whole family when we were there. Then Pop and I went again in 1968, after my mam was gone. And Pop and I went once to Australia to visit in the early 1980s.

58.

PASSING YEARS

On September 23, 1985, in Utrecht, The Netherlands, Bertus Cornelis Flissinger died at the age of sixty-five. He had had careers as a wheeled vehicle mechanic, an administrator of stock records, and as a chief internal auditor.

Five months later his wife, Clara Olivia (Ollie) Carter Flissinger, followed on February 20, 1986 in the same city. She was fifty-nine and she and Bert had been married for thirty-eight years.

****

On April 30, 1987, in Penrith, New South Wales, Australia, Jacobus (Ko) Martinus Flissinger succumbed at sixty-two. In addition to his train career Ko had been an avid practitioner and instructor in acupuncture.

****

On July 1, 1988, Marie Johanna Luikens Klein, eighty-one, died in Velp, The Netherlands.

****

On May 23, 1991, Albertina Hermanna Luikens - Sister Jacqueline - passed away in Schyndel, The Netherlands, at the age of eight-five. That same year, on October 6, her sister, Johanna Jacoba (Jopie) Luikens also passed. She was seventy-seven and living in Leiden, The Netherlands.

****

On March 5, 1995, while on another visit to his home country, Roeland (Boetie) van der Torren was unexpectedly taken in Jakarta at age sixty-two. His second wife, Eugenie, was with him and buried him in the nearby city of Bepok.

****

On December 3, 1999, in Nymegen, The Netherlands, Marie van der Torren Luikens, since 1946 the widow of Wolter Luikens, Rika's brother, passed away at age ninety.

****

On March 4, 2000, Ko's wife, Leoni Mary van Buuren Flissinger, seventy-five years old, died in Valley Heights, New South Wales, Australia.

****

On August 10, 2001, René's wife, Rhonda Constance Feutrill Flissinger passed at seventy-seven in Penrith, New South Wales, Australia.

59.

NOBLE LIVES

Maja, Barry, Frederika, Ernest, Frank, and Ray
at the turn of the century

For some loved ones to be significantly recognized and honored it sometimes takes a book like this. It affords a detailed description of their journeys and intimate portrayals of their characters and constitutions. It also allows for a much deeper look into their hearts and souls, what made them who they are, and what effect they had on others. With enough delving and the particulars sufficiently enumerated, when all is said and done, "legacy" is brought to mind and fittingly enwraps the totality. Ernest and Frederika have certainly left an indelible mark for younger generations to revere and treasure.

On May 23, 2006, Ernest fell in his home. Frederika, Maja, and Ray were on hand to facilitate his being taken to the hospital. There it was determined that he had suffered a stroke. The rest of his family was notified and before long all the children, grandchildren, and great-grandchildren, plus Wolter and Nora van der Torren and family, came to visit him.

For the next twelve days a family member was always by his side. Frederika sat vigilantly with him every day. Some days Ernest showed small signs of improvement, but most indications were not positive.

On June 4, Ernest Hubert Flissinger passed away at the age of eighty-eight. Frederika and son Frank were at his side. His other children arrived within minutes.

It is extremely difficult to imagine the loss Frederika must have felt. She has never been one to wear her emotions on her sleeve and the strength that she displayed throughout her whole life likely supported her in that moment and in the weeks and months and years that have followed. Just suffice it to remember that she and Ernest knew each other for seventy years and were married for sixty-four.

And how do you say good-bye to a parent who has been in your life as long as you have been alive? Maja, Ray,

Barry, and Frank were blessed to have had their father all their years.

Ernest was survived by his wife, four children, eight grandchildren, and six great-grandchildren. A handsome urn box now holds the ashes of this cherished man, in quiet anticipation of the matrimony with Frederika's ashes when the time arrives.

The day after her father's passing, Maja stumbled upon a greeting card in her parents' home. It was a Father's Day card from the mid-1960s, before any of the children were married, from the whole family to Ernest. Maja was understandably moved by her discovery. Upon her suggestion, this author was inspired to expand the card's sentiment into the poem now affixed to the urn, paying ardent tribute to the noble couple.

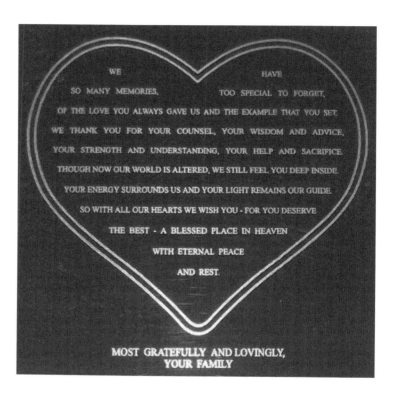

WE   HAVE

SO MANY MEMORIES,   TOO SPECIAL TO FORGET,

OF THE LOVE YOU ALWAYS GAVE US AND THE EXAMPLE THAT YOU SET.

WE THANK YOU FOR YOUR COUNSEL, YOUR WISDOM AND ADVICE,

YOUR STRENGTH AND UNDERSTANDING, YOUR HELP AND SACRIFICE.

THOUGH NOW OUR WORLD IS ALTERED, WE STILL FEEL YOU DEEP INSIDE.

YOUR ENERGY SURROUNDS US AND YOUR LIGHT REMAINS OUR GUIDE.

SO WITH ALL OUR HEARTS WE WISH YOU - FOR YOU DESERVE

THE BEST - A BLESSED PLACE IN HEAVEN

WITH ETERNAL PEACE

AND REST.

**MOST GRATEFULLY AND LOVINGLY,
YOUR FAMILY**

⁎⁎

Ernest had, on several occasions as far back as the late 1950s, mentioned to his daughter that before he died he wanted to build a small chapel in the mountains for Jesus's beloved Mother Mary. He pictured it on a hill somewhere where people could go to pray. The project never materialized for Ernest, but following her father's death, Maja felt an ambition to make it happen for him.

Maja contacted her local Catholic cemetery in Sacramento and asked what options were available. She proposed a small statue of Mary. This cemetery's rules, however, only permitted full-size statues, quite costly.

The administrator then proffered the idea of a bench. Maja was aware that there were granite benches on display around the property in obvious reverence to some dear departed, but she did not feel such a monument would be a suitable alternative for her father's vision. But the administrator pointed out a bench that was available, already in place in a very prominent, centrally located position. To Maja's amazement the bench's site was directly across from the cemetery chapel and also in front of a replicated sculpture of the "Pieta" - Mother Mary holding the body of Jesus! It wasn't a chapel on a hill, but how closely and wonderfully it fulfilled Ernest's dream!

On June 24, 2007, in the presence of her mother and many family members and friends, Maja ceremoniously dedicated the bench, complete with images and engraving, to her loving parents.

The miraculous story of Ernest and Frederika Flissinger could not have a more fitting ending than to have its final words etched in stone.

60.

EPILOGUE: ONCE UPON A PARADISE

The center of Ernest and Frederika's universe and the foundation of their happiness has always been family. They often expressed how important they felt it was to keep family close. Knowing where they came from and how they lived, it's easy to understand and appreciate their philosophy.

It has been a pleasure for the whole family through the years to listen to these elders recount their young lives and the good times they enjoyed in the Dutch East Indies. It has also been heart-breaking to hear of the hardship and misfortune they and their families and so many other islanders suffered. We can never fully comprehend the enormity of their experience, but we can be ever so grateful - not to mention, amazed - that the sweet has outweighed the sour and that Nes and Rika managed to live long and prosperously and with an overall affable and positive approach to life.

> FF: We made a good choice to move to America. We had a tough time here for a few years, but it turned out to be the right decision.

EF: Looking back on it, we survived all the miseries. The atrocities that took place during the Japanese occupation and during the native uprising were indescribable. All I can say – extremely cruel. We haven't been back to Indonesia.

Because Ernest and Frederika have shared their stories of the land on the other side of the earth, our lives are enriched and our hearts are fuller. Beauty is not always just in the eye of the beholder. It can also most certainly be in the mind of the listener.

EF: Indonesia is the most beautiful country I've ever seen. We've traveled all over the world, Rika and I, and I can make comparison. There are many beautiful countries, but I still favor Indonesia.

**

In retirement Frederika, the beneficiary of sound investments and the continuing installments of Ernest's monthly pension from The Netherlands, still lives in the comfort of her own home. Son Ray resides with her and Maja and Frank are on call at a moment's notice (Barry is nearby, too, though his health is at issue). At ninety-seven Rika continues to enjoy cooking and occasionally playing the piano. In relatively good health, our matriarch - the last living family member of her generation on either side - avidly watches TV and works diligently on cryptograms to keep her mind sharp. And she is still generous with assistance to her family when needs arise.

For many decades Ernest Flissinger had carried in a small leather pouch in his pocket the rosary that Father Molenaar had given him. It was one of Ernest's most treasured possessions, as it had helped him through many a desperate circumstance and brought him great comfort. "Rome" was embossed on the back of the cross, suggesting its place of origin, and in addition to the rosary's outward beauty and symbolism, inside the cross was a splinter of wood believed to be from the cross of Christ. When one of Ernest's children fell ill, he would open the cross and have the ailing youngster touch the splinter. There was even a time in the early 1960s when the rosary was lost. After putting a notice in a local newspaper, Ernest was jubilant when informed that someone had found and returned it, the deed once again typifying the goodness the Flissingers had come to appreciate in the American character. But through the years the beaded chain had required repair. It finally fell apart to the extent it could not be restored. Not disheartened, Ernest mounted the rosary's cross on a pin and continued to wear it on his undershirt each and every day.

Frederika now wears Ernest's cross on a chain around her neck, right next to the locket encasing her father's picture, which she has been wearing every day since her mother gave it to her in 1922.

Rika also cherishes a Teddy bear she still possesses from her childhood. It was the last gift her father gave her.

FREDERIKA IN 2013

APPENDIXES

EPIC POEM

The following poem, stanzas 1-12, completed November 17, 1996, was composed by Marguerite J. Flissinger-Gavin and Matt Gavin. It is based on the idea, remembrances, and information compiled by Marguerite for the celebration of Frederika Flissinger's 80th birthday and Ernest Flissinger's 79th birthday in November of that year.

Stanza 13 was added December 25, 2005, to update the story as of that date. Stanza 14 was added December 25, 2009, once again to update the story. Due to the completion of this book (2013) and the natural progression of family members' lives, it is appropriate to add Stanza 15 this year.

THE VERY BLESSED

1.

Once upon an autumntime, the Luikenses sailed the seas
Aboard a steamer bound for islands called the East Indies.
The past six months a furlough earned, away from Shell Oil's chores,
Allowed dear times in Holland, their beloved native shores.

The year was 1916 then - perhaps they'd best be gone.
All Europe was in turmoil, for the First Great War was on.
But Mr. L. had more concerns - his wife was long with child.
Would sailing halfway 'round the world be all too rough and wild?

The best advice - to stay behind - fell deaf on mother's ears.
To be apart from those she loved was worse than all the fears.
So man and wife, with children five, braved "what would be would be",
And all on board, the captain too, kept vigil anxiously.

But this is all a happy tale, so don't for once dismay.
In mid-November's briny chill they reached the Biscay Bay.
And there upon the ocean blue, with joyful spank and cry,
Another girl, Frederika named, came forth to greet the sky!

2.

Now, unbeknownst to these dear folks, another Holland clan,
Whose head was also Dutch-assigned - a leading postal man,
Lived there as well on Indies soil, on Java, as it were,
And carried proudly in those parts the name of Flissinger.

This family, too, was offspring-bent, and now in '17,
As mid-November neared again, another face was seen.
A second son, of six all told, Ernest, well-named, arrived,
And toughing out a malady, against the odds survived.

So "Nes" and "Rika" grew and played in tropic pleasures rife.
They loved the mountains, waters clear, the birds and wildlife.
They learned proficiently at school, spoke island tongues as well,
Preparing them for life's events of which the years would tell.

As time marched on their families were known to change address,
And hero and sweet heroine reached middle teens, no less.
And then, perhaps by happenstance - or kismet from the start -
The Luikenses and Flissingers now lived one house apart!

235

3.

Young folks' minds from early on are filled with dreams and drives.
Where will they go, what will they do, for value to their lives?
Since Rika loved her lessons so, one path was readymade.
She chose to teach in local schools, a fine and worthy trade.

Policemen's work, though perilous, is full of great intrigue.
Ernest, with wits and boxing skill, was primed to join this league.
Though slight of build, the peoplesense he had was more than most,
And after testing numerous times, at last he won a post.

But young men's fancies in the spring turn amorous, we know,
And love can cause a mighty stir and change a course's flow.
While focus seemed to be upon horizons to explore,
Ernest was keeping yet one eye on the dark-haired girl next door.

Back then a courtship of some length was proper, dignified.
So Nes wooed Rika six sweet years, till minds and hearts allied.
Then down the aisle, in '42, they joyfully made their way
And vowed their love forevermore, that memorable Sixth of May.

4.

The '40s brought so many days and years of consequence.
The newlyweds will not forget the harsh experience.
The Second War "to end all wars" engulfed the world clear 'round.
But now is not the prudent time the details to expound.

Despite the war new nuptial bliss brought changes for the good.
In '45, our bride and groom embarked on parenthood!
A daughter, Marguerite, was born - called Maja - soon that spring.
And so began the lifelong joys of care and nurturing.

Ernest (now Pop!) stayed hard at work, each crime was so involved.
But soon his name grew legend there with every case he solved.
And Mom continued teaching school, this double-duty spouse,
While raising up their little girl and keeping home and house.

The trio island-hopped as occupation needs arose.
But family life is full of change, as every parent knows.
By Christmas '46 and '8, the three were twicemore blessed.
The stork (or cockatoo!) brought Ray and Barry to the nest!

5.

The Indonesian postwar years were fraught with ill events.
Disdain was constantly displayed toward foreign governments.
Now safety for his family first was ever on Pop's mind,
And thoughts came often to his head to leave these woes behind.

But then as if a wand were waved or stars aligned just right,
A clergyman the family knew resolved their anxious plight.
His kin agreed to sponsor them - though miles across the sea -
And all at once America was in their destiny!

December, 1951 was filled with fond farewells.
Then once again a steamer, large, cut through the ocean swells
To the land renowned for giving help, a chance for one and all.
As the new year ushered in great hope, Miss Liberty stood tall!

But their sponsor lived as yet 3000 tiring miles from there.
They'd heard of California, yes, but Sacramento - where?
A train ride finally brought them "home", but apprehension came -
These immigrants had only thirty dollars to their name.

6.

They'd made it to the "promised land", home of the free and brave.
But now compared to island life their prospects seemed quite grave.
What would they do? Would this whole move be just one big regret?
A ranch hand was the luck of draw - how American can you get!

Pop toiled long each working day, whatever the demand,
While Mom and kids took shelter there upon the owner's land.
It was so fruitless, or it seemed, these months of sweated brow,
But as their English grasp improved they inched ahead somehow.

Then Mr. Slakey came along to give luck's bowl a stir.
In plumbing works, he took a shine to an honest foreigner.
Thus "Ernie" learned the company game and carried quite a load.
So good he was at selling parts, they sent him on the road.

And fortune turned, as well it should for those who struggle hard.
The family found a house to buy, not big, but with a yard!
Though not so plush or fancy-styled, it was, they felt, a gem,
For it was theirs and, thank the Lord, at last a home for them.

7.

Those days were tough, to say the least, but time is medicine.
The children romped and went to school and learned "American".
And family first - the bond - relieved all cares the family bore.
As evidence, young Frank was born in June of '54.

But Pop's one income left a bit desired when day was done,
So Mom earned at a cannery. Tomatoes, anyone?
Then laundries counted her a strength among their personnel,
And tired, but grateful, every night, the couple slept quite well.

Rika next took forward steps to earn a better wage.
She grabbed the opportunity to join the computer age.
While still she juggled keeping house and raising children, too,
A Department of Employment job would suit her fine, thank you.

It took five long and grueling years to end their odyssey.
In no small way the Flissingers had whipped adversity.
It felt like this had been a test they could have failed but passed.
They earned the name, Americans - proud citizens at last!

8.

A car with fins, a picket fence, and evenings with TV!
Prosperity was on the rise from sea to shining sea.
The songs bespoke of purest love and feelings were true blue.
The '50s were the sweetest times the U.S. ever knew.

With car and house and TV set and each a firm career,
Nes and Rika found their life grew better by the year.
Though not exactly duplicating Ozzie/Harriet,
To say they knew the American dream assuredly would fit.

Too quickly though, with age it seems, the seasons hurry by.
The kids turned into teenagers with graduations nigh.
Despite the parent-offspring ties, each fledgling, on its own,
Must leave the nest, when time is right, and try its wings alone.

First Maja joined with old Ma Bell and got a pal roommate.
Ray went to college, on to 'Nam, then teamed up with the state.
And Barry and young brother Frank - good plumbing work they found.
Then all to Maja bid farewell as she was L.A. bound.

238

9.

With progeny out of the house sometimes the blues await,
For dads and moms may feel the pangs the empty nests create.
Around the Flissinger abode, this hardly was the case.
The sound of little feet was never absent from the place.

From hearty stock the men it seemed were predisposed to wed.
Into the fold dear ladies came and nuptial vows were said.
Diane and Alice, Kathy, too; Roberta down the line.
The family tree began to branch in 1969.

A boy named Corey started things, the first to steal the show,
Then Tara, Geoffrey, Phillip, came, and Megan in a row,
Plus David, Nicky, not blood-tied, still family, no mistake,
And Ashley, Tyler, Melanie. Oh, what a group they make!

In "Oma", "Opa" heartstrings tugged as each new life unfurled.
It brought a fresh and sweet and "grand" perspective to their world.
This passing on of family genes - when all is done and said -
Perhaps there is no better way for love on earth to spread.

10.

There was a very special knack that flowed through Nes's veins.
He had a gift for salesmanship, as history now maintains.
He read so well a person's quirks - he'd learned that as a cop -
For years his productivity was rated at the top.

Now he had the luxury of surplus funds to use,
And real estate appeared the wise investment plan to choose.
With Oma's sharp arithmetic, they were a clever pair,
And over time they made a pretty penny here and there.

They bought a house on Jamestown Drive, to move a bit upscale,
And land in various locales, with thoughts of future sale,
And just for leisure for themselves and the family as it grew,
A house atop a foothill ridge, and a lot with ocean view.

By the early '80s they had reached a certain pinnacle.
They had few needs or wants or cares, their lives were very full.
They'd done their work and earned their pay for decades as required.
Then one sweet day, without fanfare, they happily retired!

11.

The golden years should be replete with fun and whims galore.
For Oma and for Opa, too, it's been that way, and more.
They love to read and watch TV and keep their knowledge keen,
Take little jaunts to nearby sites to see what can be seen.

Oma listens to her tunes, plays piano melodies,
And still prepares her famous meals, her island recipes.
Her rijstaafel, for special days, is nothing short of great,
And New Year's spek coek, what a treat, is worth the yearly wait!

Opa loves the out of doors, the yard, his trees and plants.
He's passionate for living things from dinosaurs to ants.
In different times he might have sought a medical degree -
He's very handy (footsy, too!) with reflexology.

Through traveling this couple's dreams have long been satisfied.
They've toured the many famous lands on continents worldwide.
But they know where their hearts remain, they readily admit.
It's still a joy to be at home - oh, yes, and babysit!

12.

We eye the new millennium with reasons to rejoice.
Most people of the world, at last, are free to speak their voice.
The Flissingers can also praise the '90s loud and strong.
For one, their daughter Maja's back, with husband Matt along.

But even more significant, in terms of family pride,
Is Corey's life with Carole now, the newest family bride.
For Christopher and Casey, too, are here to stake their claim,
Another generation born to carry on the name.

Throughout their lives these caring folks have tried to make it sure
That no one was in dire need, that the family stayed secure.
Like second nature, maybe first, they've never thought to stop
The flow of love and nurturing - their roles as Mom and Pop.

And now their span of eighty years is what we celebrate,
So grateful for our time with them and for their healthy state.
Our birthday wish for both is that all people near and far
Should know - as we have for so long - how wonderful they are!

13.

Time has a way, for some at least, of being kind and fair.
This tale, you see, is far from done, about this blessed pair.
Mom's eighty-nine, Pop's eighty-eight - it's now 2005.
With thanks to God and love and luck the Flissingers still thrive.

The family tree is growing strong with branches ever green.
New names and faces have appeared to charm the kindred scene.
It's Ray and Agnes, arm in arm, who foxtrot, waltz, and swing.
And Racheal is Goeff's sweet, new love, with wedding bells to ring.

There's Megan with her Mario and strapping sons to rear.
First Payton came, then Mason, too, to spread the household cheer.
For Corey and for Carole now young Collin gives them three.
And Tara's wed to Cameron, with little Grace at knee.

So, long with life these parents dear, still healthy in most ways,
Take pleasure yet in memories and special family days.
Though time on earth is short, we know, our spirits don't lose sight -
We count our blessings every day - for past - and future bright.

14.

We add these words, though bittersweet, this year 2009.
The Flissingers, heart-wrenched, lament a light that fails to shine.
For mortals live a finite time upon this spinning sphere,
And finally love and memories are all that keep them near.

Our Pop, dear Ernest, patriarch, who loved his family so,
Passed over to his great reward in June three years ago.
But energy like his on earth is universe-aligned
And lingers strong as life goes forth for those now left behind.

In balance to this heavy loss came merriment as well.
The year that followed heralded more birthing news to tell.
To Geoff and Racheal's sweet delight came Vinson - what a boy!
And Mario and Megan added Mia to their joy!

Now Frederika, ninety-three, is matriarch sole-crowned.
And a bench, engraved with family lore, sits high on Catholic ground.
It basks, per Maja's fine design, in California's sun,
To honor Pop and Mom always for all that they have done.

15.

The annals mount and bring us to two thousand and thirteen.
The march of time has led, of course, to changes unforeseen.
Not every turn is positive, to state the likelihood,
But to our joy the news, to date, continues to be good.

More grandchildren have ventured out: to Carl is Ashley wed;
With college courses Melanie's and Tyler's fires are fed;
While Phillip serves our country well, our freedoms to uphold,
His marriage brings nurse Brittney with young Ava to the fold.

The great-grandchildren, nine in all, with worlds still at their door,
Spurt ever upward toward their dreams, inspired by those before.
As older generations watch the younger ones hold sway,
Dear Frederika adds a year – her ninety-seventh! Yea!

And these days gracing family shelves a book, forever bound,
Recounts the tale of two of note whose impact was profound.
It narrates Nes and Rika's life, from vast remembrances,
And celebrates the wondrous pair. A fine tribute, it is!

16.

Even sagas, decades long, come naturally to "The End",
But here this storied trek has just a bit more path to wend.
This tale of two young islanders whose lives were very blessed
Relates one final marked event to consummate the rest.

Dear Rika, under children's watch, lived long another role -
Her generation's Flissinger and Luikens final soul.
Then March the 7th, 2015, nine years since Nes had passed,
At ninety-eight, "I love you all!" – she peacefully breathed her last.

But legacies do carry on and family trees branch new.
Now Ray has Lori, fiancée, Briana, Bianca, too.
And Phillip and his Brittney proud have borne sweet manly fruit.
First Rylan came to warm their hearts, then Ronan followed suit.

It has been said that history's like a great enlightening sage,
And words have consequential might when penned upon the page.
If such is true, the world has gained from Nes and Rika's time,
And TWO TO BE REMEMBERED is – for strength – a paradigm.

LINEAGE OF

ERNEST HUBERT FLISSINGER

ANTHONY COENRAAD FLISSINGER b. __ / __ / 1831 Surabaya, Java

d. __ / __ / 1883 Surabaya, Java

m. __ / __ / ____ city unk.

HENDRIKA CHRISTINA CRAMER b. __ / __ / ____ city unk.

d. __ / __ / ____ city unk.

children:

Antoinette Charlotte Flissinger b. __ / __ / ____ city unk.

d. __ / __ / ____ city unk.

Dora Flissinger b. __ / __ / ____ city unk.

d. __ / __ / ____ city unk.

Heinrich Flissinger b. __ / __ / ____ city unk.

d. __ / __ / ____ city unk.

|------FREDERICH WILHELM FLISSINGER

| Marie Flissinger b. __ / __ / ____ city unk.

| d. __ / __ / ____ city unk.

| Ketelaar Flissinger b. __ / __ / ____ city unk.

| d. __ / __ / ____ city unk.

|

|

FREDERICH WILHELM FLISSINGER b. 12/15/1862 Surabaya, Java

                                    d. 12/19/____   city unk.

    m. 5/5/1884 Surabaya, Java

    div. 1902 (Rosalie)

    re-m. 3/21/1923 (Rosalie)

    ROSALIE CRAMER   b. 10/22/1867 Modjokerto, Java

                                      d. 9/23/1938   Surabaya, Java

        children:

        Edward Flissinger   b. __ /__ /____ city unk.

                                 d. __ /__ /____ city unk.

        Laurence Flissinger   b. __ /__ /____ city unk.

                                 d. __ /__ /____ city unk.

        Jeanne Flissinger   b. __ /__ /____ city unk.

                                 d. __ /__ /____ city unk.

| ------FRANS WILLEM FLISSINGER

| Jan Flissinger   b. __ /__ /____ city unk.

| d. __ /__ /____ city unk.

|

FRANS WILLEM FLISSINGER   b. 6/8/1888   Surabaya, Java

                                      d. 6/8/1951   Jakarta, Java

m. __ / __ / 1909 Surabaya, Java

<u>MARTINA JACOBA ADRIANA BROENS</u>

	b. 6/11/1892	Delft, Netherlands
	d. 4/13/1956	Valley Heights, N.S.W., Australia

children:

Frances Flissinger	b. __ / __ / ____	city unk.
	d. __ / __ / ____	Atjeh, Sumatra
Agatha Flissinger	b. __ / __ / ____	Atjeh, Sumatra
	d. __ / __ / ____	Atjeh, Sumatra
Willem Rudolf Flissinger	b. 9/16/1916	Batavia, Java
	d. __ / __ / 1943	Seram, Indonesia

| ------ERNEST HUIBERT FLISSINGER

|	René Adolf Flissinger	b. 4/27/1919	Bangil, East Java
|		d. 6/11/1976	St. Marys, N.S.W., Australia
|	Bertus Cornelis Flissinger	b. 9/1/1920	Bangil, East Java
|		d. 9/23/1985	Utrecht, The Netherlands
|	Jacobus Martinus Flissinger	b. 11/20/1924	Djombang, Java.
|		d. 4/30/1987	Penrith, N.S.W., Australia
|	Martinus Jacobus Flissinger	b. 6/6/1929	Bandung, Java
|		d. 8/20/1936	Batavia, Java

245

|	[daughter - died at birth]	b. __ / __ / 1939	Batavia, Java
|		d. __ / __ / 1939	Batavia, Java
|			

ERNEST HUIBERT (HUBERT) FLISSINGER

	b. 11/9/1917	Batavia, Java
	d. 6/4/2006	Sacramento, California, U.S.A.

m. 5/6/1942 Jakarta, Java

FREDERIKA ADRIANA LUIKENS   b. 11/18/1916   Bay of Biscay (aboard ship)

children:

Marguerite Jacqueline Flissinger

        b. 3/14/1945   Jakarta, Java

Raymond Ernest Everhart Flissinger

        b. 12/19/1946   Ambon, Indonesia

Bartholomeus Sylvester Flissinger

        b. 12/14/1948   Ambon, Indonesia

Francis John Flissinger   b. 6/15/1954   Sacramento, California, U.S.A.

LINEAGE OF
MARTINA JACOBA ADRIANA BROENS

<u>JACOBUS PETRUS BROENS</u>   b. 7/25/1858   city unk.
The Netherlands

d. 5/25/1900   Surabaya, E.Java

m. __/__/____ city unk., The Netherlands

<u>ADRIANA JACOBA AGATHA CALVIS</u>

b. 7/25/1863   city unk.

d. 3/22/1910   Surabaya, E.Java

child:

|------MARTINA JACOBA ADRIANA BROENS

|

<u>MARTINA JACOBA ADRIANA BROENS</u>

b. 6/11/1892   Delft, Netherlands

d. 4/13/1956   Valley Heights,
N.S.W., Australia

m. __ /__ /1909 Surabaya, Java

<u>FRANS WILLEM FLISSINGER</u>   b. 6/8/1888   Surabaya, E.Java

d. 6/8/1951   Jakarta, Java

LINEAGE OF

FREDERIKA ADRIANA LUIKENS

<u>WOLTER LUKENS</u>   b. __ / __ /1837 Pekela,
                    The Netherlands

               d. __ / __ / ____ city unk.

  m. 2/2/1860 Pekela, The Netherlands

<u>JAPIER NIEBOER</u>   b. 10/15/1840 Pekela,
                    The Netherlands

               d. __ / __ / ____ Rio de Janeiro,
                    Brazil

  children:

  Hermanna Wendolina Lukens b. __ / __ / ____ Pekela,
                    The Netherlands

               d. __ / __ / ____ city unk.

  Margriet Lukens   b. __ / __ / ____ Pekela,
                    The Netherlands

               d. __ / __ / ____ city unk.

|------JOHANNES LUKENS

| Jan Lukens   b. __ / __ / ____ Pekela,
                    The Netherlands

| d. __ / __ / ____ city unk.

|

|

<u>JOHANNES LUIKENS</u>   b. 11/30/1865 Pekela,
                                              The Netherlands

                              d. 1/8/1922   Palembang,
                                              Sumatra

m. __ / __ / 1902 Batavia, Java

<u>MARIE JACQUELINE de la FONTEYNE</u>

                              b. 1/16/1883   Batavia, Java

                              d. 2/16/1966   Nymegen,
                                              The Netherlands

children:

Albertina Hermanna Luikens   b. 7/8/1905   Batavia, Java

                              d. 5/23/1991   Schyndel,
                                              The Netherlands

Maria Johanna Luikens   b. 6/2/1907   Palembang,
                                              Sumatra

                              d. 7/1/1988   Velp, Netherlands

Wolter Franciscus Luikens   b. 8/27/1909   Palembang,
                                              Sumatra

                              d. 4/13/1946   Jakarta, Java

Sophia Antonia Luikens   b. 8/1/1911   Palembang,
                                              Sumatra

                              d. 7/27/1943   Jakarta, Java

Johanna Jacoba Luikens   b. 11/8/1913   Palembang,
                                              Sumatra
                              d. 10/6/1991   Leiden,
                                              The Netherlands

| ------FREDERIKA ADRIANA LUIKENS

| Jantje Luikens   b. 1/11/1922   Palembang, Sumatra

| d. 1/12/1922   Palembang, Sumatra

|

FREDERIKA ADRIANA LUIKENS   b. 11/18/1916   Bay of Biscay (aboard ship)

     m. 5/6/1942 Jakarta, Java

     ERNEST HUBERT FLISSINGER   b. 11/9/1917   Batavia, Java

                                           d. 6/4/2006   Sacramento, California, U.S.A.

LINEAGE OF
MARIE JACQUELINE
DE LA FONTEYNE

<u>FRANCISCUS JACOBUS de la FONTEYNE</u>

	b. 10/3/1932	Vlissingen, The Netherlands
	d. 3/8/1922	Den Helder, The Netherlands

m. __ / __ / ____ city unk.

<u>SIELA</u>

	b. __ / __ / ____	city unk.
	d. __ / __ / ____	city unk.

    children:

|------FRANCISCUS ANTON EVERHARD de la FONTEYNE

| Frederika de la Fonteyne   b. __ / __ / ____   city unk.

| d. __ / __ / ____   city unk.

|

<u>FRANCISCUS ANTON EVERHARD de la FONTEYNE</u>

	b. 2/16/1856	Sambas, Borneo
	d. 8/__ /1923	Batavia, Java

m. __ / __ /circa 1880 city unk.

251

ALBERTINA CAROLINE HERMAN   b. 4/22/1861   Ambarawa, Java

                                        d. 8/1/1901   Batavia, Java

       children:

       Albertina de la Fonteyne   b. __ / __ / ____   city unk.

                                          d. __ / __ / ____   city unk.

|------MARIE JACQUELINE de la FONTEYNE

| Frederick Eduard de la Fonteyne

| b. 3/14/1885   Oenaran, Java

| d. __ / __ / ____   city unk.

| Sophia de la Fonteyne   b. __ / __ / ____   city unk.

| d. __ / __ / ____   city unk.

| Alex de la Fonteyne   b. __ / __ / ____   city unk.

| d. __ / __ / ____   city unk.

|

MARIE JACQUELINE de la FONTEYNE

                                        b. 1/16/1883   Batavia, Java

                                        d. 2/16/1966   Nymegen,
                                                             The Netherlands

     m. __/__/1902 Batavia, Java

JOHANNES LUIKENS   b. 11/30/1865 Pekela,
                                                   The Netherlands

                                        d. 1/8/1922   Palembang,
                                                             Sumatra

ABOUT THE AUTHOR

Matt Gavin thrived on a nurturing family upbringing in New Jersey, Missouri, and North Carolina. At a young age the Broadway musicals and light operas in his parents' record collection captivated his interest. He began writing poems and lyrics before he was a teenager, and other burgeoning talents gave him opportunities to perform as a vocalist and a clarinetist throughout junior high and high school. In continued pursuit of performance dreams Matt graduated from the University of Cincinnati College-Conservatory of Music in voice and choral music.

After brief acting stints in dinner theater, summer stock, and regional theater, Matt excitedly moved to New York City, and in a surprisingly short time he was chosen to be in a Broadway musical (the original cast of "Shenandoah", 1975)! During the show's two-and-a-half-year run, Matt had abundant time to practice another craft. He delighted in learning how to put his original ideas for songs, stage productions, and television on the printed page. But he also came to learn that acting careers are built on continually landing jobs, and that was not his good fortune. Like many before him, Matt decided to try Hollywood.

Los Angeles turned out to be an extraordinary adventure. Even though his quest for a lucrative acting career turned out to be fruitless, the comfortable climate and the Hollywood energy proved extremely conducive for inspiration. Matt wrote sit-coms, TV movies, feature films, and more songs. Although he never sold any of them, with each effort he honed his skills and cherished the imaginative process all the more.

In 1981 Matt met Maja Flissinger in North Hollywood. A second-time-around relationship brought them beautifully to the altar there in 1991. Life in L.A. still held some allure, but then Mother Nature came calling. The 1994 Northridge earthquake transformed the couple's view of things. Nothing was anchoring them in southern California any longer and Maja's parents were in advanced age. Relocating to Sacramento was an intriguing and logical choice. It turned out to be a very gratifying move.

Matt spent most of his post-acting, pre-retirement days in accounting, hotel, and retail work. But all the while he continued with his love for writing. In 2011, one of his screenplays won first place in a national contest. Though until now he has not been published or produced, Matt's joy in being creative has not diminished. He relishes every opportunity to write, and he feels extremely grateful to have been at the right place and right time to author this memorable story of the Flissingers and Luikens.

Made in the USA
Columbia, SC
17 March 2020

89246464R00148